SUZY CHIAZZARI

THE HEALING HOME

SUZY CHIAZZARI

THE HEALING HOME

CREATING THE PERFECT PLACE TO LIVE

WITH COLOUR, AROMA, LIGHT

AND OTHER NATURAL ELEMENTS

Trafalgar Square Publishing

First published in the United States of America in 1998 by

Trafalgar Square Publishing, North Pomfret, Vermont 05053

First paperback edition 2000

Printed and bound in Singapore by Tien Wah Press

1 3 5 7 9 10 8 6 4 2

First published in the United Kingdom in 1998 by Ebury Press

ISBN 1-57076-160-4

Library of Congress Catalog Card Number: 99-65358

Editor Emma Callery
Designer Ruth Prentice
Picture research Nadine Bazar

Contents

Introduction – The Loving Home

The home is a place to be loved and a place for loving. It provides a sense of belonging, affection and togetherness. Since ancient times we have always found a place where we preferred to be, around which we could structure our lives. This special space provides shelter from the elements and satisfies the deep longing of our soul to dwell in a place which is healthy for the body, mind and spirit. Our home is therefore a spiritual place which links us to the earth, our environment and the community. It is somewhere we begin and end the day, and where at one time we would have been born and eventually died.

With the changes in our social structures and way of life, our spiritual links with our home have slowly become eroded. Since the modern movement in architecture in the twenties and thirties, houses have been designed more to make the most of modern building materials and advances in technology than they have for the people who will live in them. We now know that while it is useful to have modern conveniences, it is no longer appropriate to build houses which are merely 'machines for living in'. To meet our changing needs for the twenty-first century, we must once again create an intimate and emotional connection with our home.

Love in its true sense is not just a subjective feeling but a celebration of being alive, and a series of actions that convey support and care. Offering your home, your time and energy will create a loving atmosphere which will be reflected back to you. So loving homes create an energy field which can nourish and feed our soul and by so doing help us develop self-love and a loving relationship with others.

Very few people can say that they are living in their ideal home, but this should not stop us making our present abode a special and loving place. Harmony in our home should never be considered a luxury and every home, no matter how humble, can be filled with loving vibrations.

In these stressful times we turn to our home to provide a haven for peace and tranquillity. This nurturing environment provides support for our outer social and inner personal harmony and provides the framework around which we can organize and color our daily lives.

If we are to create a home which will nurture all that is best in the human spirit we also need to make sure our home has empathy with its surroundings.

Very few houses built today take into account the natural landscape and spiritual traditions of the past. The trend towards attaining material wealth and possessions has been so ingrained into us, that we have forgotten that there are other, more important, goals in life. The home is a reflection of these attitudes and ideals, and the concern with superficial appearances and impressions has seen the house become a statement of status and social position. This is why many modern buildings dominate and alienate the landscape and natural environment as well as making the occupants feel separate from nature, each other and their own true spirit.

The tide has now turned as we recognize that material wealth, power and domination will never bring us peace and contentment. Many people are now endeavoring to revert to a simpler, more natural lifestyle, an essential part of which is to live in a loving, supportive home.

Unfortunately, most people cannot afford to design ecological friendly and healthy houses, and find themselves living in a space designed by a builder or architect who has already defined the shape and size of the rooms. There are, however, many ways we can improve the vital energy in a house, turning it into a loving home where we can feel peace

A DISPLAY OF AUTUMN VEGETABLES HELPS US CONNECT TO THE RHYTHM

OF THE SEASONS.

and rest. By using natural materials, full-spectrum lights, energy-balancing sounds, fragrances, fabrics and colors we can charge our home with energy that harmonizes with natural forces. By honoring the places in which we live in this way, we honor the earth, and honor ourselves.

Vital energy

Everything in this universe is composed of a mass of constantly moving energy. Atoms and molecules spin and vibrate in certain rhythms, giving matter form and shape. Thus everything on this planet is interconnected by the vibrations of life-force energy which flows between them. This means that our home, too, is composed of energy. It is not separate from us, and like us has an evolving consciousness with which we can communicate.

The vibrations found in the home can be life-suppressing or life-enhancing. Rudolph Steiner, an Austrian philosopher and founder of Anthroposophical medicine, believed that if people could be surrounded by living architectural forms and spaces, it would have a beneficial effect on their mental and physical health. He also realized how important our environment is to our social behavior and that crime and violence could be deterred by buildings with positive energy flow and color vibrations.

The existence of life-force energy has been known from ancient times and had many different names in the teachings of all the major religions. Christians refer to this spiritual force as 'The Holy Ghost', while the Hindus call this primal energy 'prana', which is attracted by and circulated through a series of energy centers in our being known as chakras.

The Chinese regard the cosmos as being pervaded by ch'i (qi) which connects the universe, the earth and our bodies through a network of lines. In the earth, this network of energy lines are known as 'laylines', while in the body they are referred to as 'meridians'.

The Taoist art of feng shui, which literally means 'wind and water', is an ancient system of placement of buildings and furniture which encourages the natural flow of vital energy or 'ch'i' through the house, thus attracting good fortune, health and happiness. Geomancy, which is now becoming popular, is a modern equivalent of feng shui, and uses dowsing to locate energetic disturbances in the ground and in buildings.

Whatever the name given to it, it is generally agreed that when this life-force energy flows harmoniously through us, connecting us to the earth, the air, each other and the other cosmic forces, we are sustained in perfect health.

The rhythms of life

When man lived close to nature he reflected these natural rhythms in his home. Every spring, the outside of the home was decorated or new earth was placed on the floor. Thatch was placed on the roof according to the cycle of the harvesting and drying of thatching grass. Moon cycles were used as signals to perform certain rites and ceremonies in the home to aid prosperity and good health.

Unfortunately, today we have lost the close connection with natural cycles. We think we need to work flat out throughout the year. Is it any wonder we burn out and weaken our body's own defense system? Our home can help us unite with the energy of the seasons, so that we can once again accept that there are natural cycles of energy throughout the year. In spring, there is a surge of energy which peaks during the longer, warmer days of summer. Autumn then heralds a slowing down and drawing in of energy which we conserve for the long winter months when we feel the least physically energetic.

There are many ways we can celebrate certain festivals and perform certain activities to remind us of the seasonal and annual cycles. Traditional spring or harvest festivals are still honored in some places, while spring cleaning the home every year is another way we can connect to the energies of each season. Summer is the season we tend to turn our attention to our gardens and outdoor living, while autumn is the time we choose for interior decorating and study projects in readiness for our winter hibernation.

Working with natural rhythms rather than against them in our homes can give our life meaning and bring fulfillment and a sense of belonging in the world.

Creating positive vibrations

When we look back at the places where we have lived during our life, we remember some with nostalgia and love while others we remember as places connected to unhappiness and pain. We often assume that the ups and downs of life are associated with the place where certain events in our life occurred. Most people leave it at that, never considering that the house and buildings themselves may have contributed to their feelings of discontentment or well-being. Buildings are essentially alive. They absorb and hold the positive and negative vibrations that circulate through them. If properly designed, they can also deflect harmful energy and radiate positive forces to the occupants and the surrounding area.

Where do these vibrations come from? Human beings are not only made up of a physical body, but have several invisible subtle bodies forming an envelope of radiant energy around us. These emanations are created by the combined vibrations of all our cells, tissues and organs, which give off electromagnetic energy in the form of light, heat, sound and color. These vibrations permeate into the air around us, affecting everything they come into contact with, including our immediate physical environment, the furniture, furnishings, walls, floors and every part of our house. If one experiences situations of great emotion or mental disturbance, these vibrations linger behind, and can often be picked up by other people at a much later date. In the same way, you may pick up vibrations from former occupants of a house.

This two-way flow of vibrational energy from us to the house and from the house back to us means that when we consciously create a peaceful and loving environment, the home will reflect these feelings. Likewise, if we consciously work at making a healing home, in times of hardship or ill health, our home will be able to emit supportive and comforting vibrations.

All things, including plants, minerals and animals, have their own auras. This includes your home. The aura of your home is made up of vibrations emitted from its physical form and pattern, the materials from which it is built, the colors and emotional thought forms pervading it, the energy from the ground and landscape surrounding it and, most of all, the love that is given and received within its walls.

The purpose of your home

Our thoughts are also vibrations, which we send out into the air around us, spreading out around us like ripples in a pond. These thought vibrations can be positive or negative, and they influence and interact with other vibrations, meaning the mind can influence other people and our environment.

Our thoughts can also influence our own well-being as they have a boomerang action. Our subtle body, known as the etheric body, picks up thought vibrations and transmits them to our physical form. In fact, the etheric body is an exact duplicate of our physical body, except it vibrates at a much higher rate, rendering it invisible to the normal eye. When a sequence of vibrating waves is set up in the etheric body, the copy-cat physical body interprets this energy and manifests it as a physical state. So, harmonious vibrations are interpreted as good health, while inharmonious ones result in ill health.

We now recognize that our state of mind has a great influence on our body's internal environment, which affects our health and general well-being. So our mind and thoughts can influence both our inner and outer environment. We can use our thoughts to help give purpose to living if we can identify our intentions when we live in a certain place. These thoughts will influence our experience of living there. Try to remember your intentions when you moved into your present home. Did you intend to stay for a short or long time? If your intention has changed, you could identify the purpose you wish to give your present home.

It is usual that when the purpose of your home has been fulfilled, you become dissatisfied with it and want to move house. At this time you need to be clear about the purpose of

UNCLUTTERED ROOMS AND THE
USE OF NATURAL MATERIALS,
LIGHT, AIR, COLOR AND PLANTS
CAN CHARGE OUR HOME WITH
VITAL ENERGY.

HEALING HOUSE RITUALS

The home can help us move smoothly from each life stage into the next. It can provide us with a focus as we progress through life. We cannot always move house when we enter a new stage but there are many ways we can create healing house rituals in harmony with natural life rhythms.

Daily and monthly rituals

- Greet the sun each morning or, if it is raining, greet the rain, the clouds, the sky.

- Find a room where the sun comes in and place a crystal ball or pendant in the window. Visit this room at a particular time each day to bathe in the beauty of the rainbows in your room.

- Burn an aromatic oil and light a candle.

- Read a few pages from a book of poetry or prayers each night.

- Try a new recipe each month using fresh food.

- Feed your pets, or wild birds, each morning and evening.

- Talk to one of your plants every day. Tell them how beautiful and wonderful they are. Tell them that they brighten up your life and watch how they grow.

- Make sure that you go into every room in your home each day. If you get a feeling of stuffiness, damp or cold, open and air the room. Every room needs your warming vibrations.

Seasonal rituals

- Spring clean your home every year. Turn out cupboards and drawers and put in fresh scented lining paper or sachets using spring aromatic oils. Wash your curtains and give your carpets a carpet shampoo using natural products.

- Hold a special dinner at the summer and winter equinox.

- Replace last year's calendar with a new one.

- Make a display of harvest vegetables and flowers.

- Plant and reap your own vegetables with the aid of a moon planting chart.

- Write a list of New Year's resolutions.

- Introduce the colors and textures of nature into your home which reflect the changing of the seasons. These could be candles, flowers and foliage, or scents which embody the quality of these times of year. In spring, choose soft colors, in summer, bright colors; in autumn, darker colors and in winter, rich ones.

- Have a housewarming anniversary party when you have been in your home one year, five years, ten years.

- Plant spring bulbs or annual flowers in a window box or in the garden.

Rituals to aid major life-changes

- Change the color of your front door when you start to feel restless.

- Hold a garage sale, selling anything you have not used for three years.

- Move your furniture around to create variety. Get rid of any pieces that have been given to you with which you do not feel comfortable.

- Buy yourself a small gift such as a picture, ornament or plant.

- Plant a tree or shrub as a ceremony for a new start and to symbolize the bringing of strength and new vitality into your life. Do this every time a new person comes to live in the house, so that you each have a plant.

- When somebody leaves the home, have a ceremony to acknowledge their departure. Clean out the room and, if possible, redecorate the room to suit its new use and occupant. Keep a photo or personal item if you wish to have good memories of the person.

- Look into a mirror and tell yourself that you are lovable and worthy of love at any age.

- Have a baby shower or baby breakfast to welcome a baby to your home.

- Hold a twenty-first birthday party and give your son or daughter a symbolic door key.

- Make a special individual aroma for a bride and groom and give them the formula so they can recreate it on their anniversary.

your new home. Your intention could be to create a home where you can bring up children safely and happily or it could be to find a place of solitude and peace.

Personal space

Our energetic envelope, known as the aura, extends outwards from our physical body in three distinguishable layers. The first layer is only a few inches (centimeters) wide, the second is 8-12 in (20-30 cm), while the third layer of our subtle bodies can extend for several yards (meters) in all directions. The aura is our greatest protector, and we need to keep it clear from interference from other people's vibrations. We all have a need for personal space, and when this space is invaded we feel a great deal of discomfort and have to withdraw to allow ourselves to breathe more freely again. You may have experienced this feeling when a stranger stands very close to you. You feel threatened and will naturally stand back. We only feel comfortable in close proximity with someone familiar or whom we like. The size of our personal space varies; some people are happy in close proximity with others, while other people require a large area in which to maneuver unencumbered. The more populated an area, the more personal space one needs. In cities and in houses where several people share a room, space is a precious commodity.

Our home is an extension of personal space. It has been described as our third skin. Our clothing represents our second skin, and our home, which resembles a cocoon or womb, acts as a further protection. The home is a place where we can retreat from the stress of the world. It is a place of privacy and refuge where we can do what we want and feel safe and secure.

Emotional attachments to places

We associate each stage in our life's journey with a different place. Our childhood home has strong memories, as do, for example, our schools, our grandparents' home, and then our first independent home.

There are seven psychological stages that we travel through during our lifetime.

These stages are childhood, early twenties, late twenties, thirties, forties, fifties, and sixties/seventies. Whatever stage you are in, the right home can help you through the soul's development and contribute to a feeling of wholeness and contentment. However, while one home may be good for someone at a certain stage, it may also be detrimental to another person in another stage. You can easily assess this by thinking about how much time you like to spend at home. If you try to go out as much as possible, it is likely that your home is not providing the right support and comfort for you. This often happens at a time when your situation has changed in some way or when your outer- and inner-selves are in conflict.

It often happens that a couple whose children have left home begin to find that the family house becomes too large and empty once they are on their own. If your partner has died, you may also feel the home cannot provide the support and harmony that you require in this new situation. Conversely, teenagers who want to expand and require their own space often find it difficult living in a home where space is shared and privacy hard to find.

Transitions between the stages in your life are as crucial as the stages themselves. In many cultures, these stages were marked with various rituals and ceremonies, because you need a clean break from each phase before you can be free to fully realize the next one. Today we have no formal transitions and it is for this reason that dissatisfaction with your home can indicate a change in your life cycle.

It may be that you have an urge to re-decorate your home, or move your furniture around, or you may wish to move house altogether. Throwing away items or storing them in an attic or garage also signals a time of inner change but at any time in your life your home can be a place where you can be replenished as you grow and change. To create a loving home which is in harmony with our natural cycles it is essential that we must first become aware of our changing needs as we progress through life.

Honoring your Home

Before houses were built in rows along streets, homes always had individual names. The name given to the house often described the intention the occupants had for their home and made the house a unique and personal place.

By giving your home a special name which best describes its personality and feeling, you can attract positive vibrations which will aid fulfillment of those intentions. Children particularly love to name rooms, so encourage them to name their own bedroom or playroom. Having a door plaque made with the child's name helps build self-esteem and gives them the feeling they have a special place in the world.

Naming ritual

Every space in your home should have a special mood and purpose. Each room or area can serve you better if you have consciously thought of its purpose by creating a special atmosphere in that place. Naming each room with a specific name acts as a reminder of the harmony which you have created and, on entering the room, its vibrations will reinforce its qualities.

Many country houses had rooms named after the color in which they were decorated. You could stay in the blue or the red room and often people would ask specifically for a certain room which they particularly liked and in which they felt comfortable. When your room has a special name and atmosphere, you immediately have an emotional relationship with it. It becomes alive and familiar.

Think of some special names for the rooms in your house and decorate them in such a way that their qualities are enhanced. Write the names on a cardboard, wooden or ceramic plaque and hang it over the door as a reminder and positive affirmation when you enter the room. Your thought waves will contribute to the healing vibrations which your home will reflect back to you.

Finding your past connections

Think now about the films you have seen, books you have read or places you have visited or want to visit. Perhaps you feel a strong pull to the mountains or sea, maybe a certain type of furniture or painting has a strong effect on you. Write down two places you feel attracted to, two colors, and two periods of history. You might also write down or draw costumes or clothing you like, list names of music or paintings you find touch your soul. It could also be a scent, like oranges or lavender, which has a strong past association for you. Particular types of food and aromas of cooking can also connect you to certain geographical places and historical periods.

Each style in the past evolved slowly with the gradual elimination of unsuitable materials or elements. Style was not artificially contrived, but rose to a peak and declined as part of a natural process. Rooms in every part of the world and throughout history developed in a manner most suitable for their time and place and best expressed its cultural flavor. Decoration and furnishings too evolved over time, fulfilling the requirements of their locale, period and occupants.

Style today has lost the essence of natural progression and is less influenced by local conditions. It draws its influences from international themes, from the global village, and develops from newly discovered materials and processes. We have since discovered that most of the methods and types of production have ignored the needs of the environment and far from creating homes of comfort and well-being, have greatly contributed to the ecological problems we have today.

This means that many people do not find a personal connection in a purely modern setting and this leaves them feeling isolated, disconnected and cold. For a room to have style and character today, it is necessary to integrate expressions of period decoration with modern elements to provide a more intimate and supportive environment.

**DIFFERENT INTENTIONS YOU MAY
HAVE FOR A HOME:**

❦ Located conveniently for
work.

❦ Allowing you space to relax
and be yourself.

❦ Beneficial to developing a
relationship.

❦ Raising a family.

❦ Healing, either emotionally
or physically.

❦ Working or from which a
special activity could be run.

A CHILD'S ROOM CAN GIVE ITS
OCCUPANT THE FEELING THAT
SHE OR HE HAS A SPECIAL PLACE
IN THE WORLD.

A truly healing home should express its own character, reflecting a modern lifestyle as well as the personality and needs of its owner. You can easily discover whether you are in a healing home if you ask yourself whether a stranger, viewing the room for the first time, would be able to state immediately what kind of person or persons live in it.

Style revivals are not a modern invention, as there have been revivals in history which became styles themselves. Through certain periods we find a search for inspiration from past cultures and different traditions. The Romans drew their inspiration from the Greeks, while the Victorians were greatly inspired by styles from the Far East as well as those from Ancient Egypt. We have reached a stage where we should not draw on historical styles merely to provide changes in fashion, but to draw us back to a simpler and more fulfilling way of life. The architectural shapes, forms and decoration used by cultures whose philosophy of life was also their way of life can help us harmonize our inner and outer house once more.

Old buildings and the subtle environment

Have you ever stopped to wonder why so many millions of people descend into country towns and villages every weekend and a growing number are leaving the cities to set up a new home and lifestyle in country areas? There is a strong drive to escape the city environment and return to a setting in keeping with human scale and a gentler way of living.

Villages that maintain a unity of traditional building style and form draw the most people, while towns where there are new housing developments and modern buildings are least popular. What attracts us to some places and not others?

Our homes are alive, pulsating with vibrations, absorbing, storing and releasing energy. They are part of the planetary ecosystem. They draw in light and heat from the sun, absorb energy from the ground, resist elements of water and wind. They also emit energy of their own, and it is this energy which radiates out from them that can assert a positive or negative pull.

Until the coming of the industrial age, people used to build homes from local materials, in harmony with the local landscape and reflecting traditional knowledge. Houses in cold climates were aligned with compass points which related to the path of the sun, so that the living rooms received the maximum warmth. The direction of the prevailing winds and natural protection of mountains, hills and trees were also taken into consideration. The sites where homes were built were chosen for their proximity to fresh air and water. Wildlife habitats and habits were investigated and honored.

Villages and towns developed as people started to build homes in clusters. Local building forms and styles developed and traditional building methods employed. The charm of traditional villages and towns is that the lines are not dead straight. Buildings are more organic and the lines of the buildings echo the curves and shapes found in nature. This is what gives such places their harmonious and unifying attraction. It is in such a place that we can feel comfortable. It connects us with the spiritual side of our being which is closely linked to other forms of life and the planet on which we live. More people are realizing, even if subconsciously, that they feel healthier, happier, and have more energy in the country.

It is for these reasons that we should try to find a home which harmonizes with the neighboring buildings and natural setting. This does not mean that all houses should be identical. In fact, variety plays an important role in making an interesting and vital place to live. Instead, we should think of a neighborhood like a piece of music. Each home is a different note each with its own quality and tone. When you combine the different notes, you create harmony and a rhythmic pattern which has a strong effect on our energetic system.

Unless a new building has been designed by an ecological architect who employs natural architecture together with a spiritual awareness it is best to try to find a home in an old building. By doing so you will be conserving land and our natural countryside, which is rapidly being eaten away by new housing developments. Most old buildings were more solidly built than modern ones, used healthier materials and provide larger and more variety of room shapes.

PICTURES AND BOOKS CAN MAKE
A STIMULATING AND
INSPIRATIONAL ENVIRONMENT,
ESPECIALLY IF YOU ARE ONE OF
THE INCREASING NUMBER OF
PEOPLE WHO WORK FROM HOME.

The Inner Home

The home is an extension of the self which tells us who we are. The type of home we live in, the style of furnishings and colors all work together to remind us of our personality, our taste, values and interests.

We often decorate our home to conform to perceived expectations from society. When we try to create a home which reflects contemporary style or a certain type of taste, it is often because we are seeking approval of a certain social group. If, on the other hand, our home reflects our own personal taste it will reflect a person who is independent and secure within. Your outer house will be in harmony with your inner house and it is then that you will enjoy a feeling of wholeness and contentment.

Our preoccupation with exterior appearances has led many people to pay attention to certain parts of their home and not to others. The more emphasis society has placed on appearances and status symbols, the more attention has been given to the front of the house and less to the other aspects. The driveway, the entrance, the 'front rooms' are all given priority, as these are the areas that neighbors, colleagues and friends will see and where they will be entertained. These are the spaces which will give the right impression. At the same time as 'front rooms' are enhanced, personal space such as rooms for sleeping, for cooking, for bathing and for children have become devalued.

Like our own body, the house is a three-dimensional structure. It has shape and form. It has a top and bottom, front, back and sides. Each part of the structure is an essential component and as important as any other. Equal love and attention needs to be given to each area if we are to enjoy balance and harmony within its walls.

If we are to bring back balance and harmony between our 'inner' and 'outer' home we need to have a better understanding of ourselves.

THIS FAMILY KITCHEN-DINER IS FILLED WITH OBJECTS THAT REFLECT THE PERSONALITY AND INTERESTS OF THE OCCUPANTS.

Our Inner House

Here are some ideas on how to interpret what you have drawn and experienced. Use your intuition when deciding which is appropriate.

✍ Strong foundations show a happy childhood or strong constitution. Solid building materials show strength of will but may also show inflexibility of thought.

✍ Did your house have a basement or cellar and what did you find there? These images symbolize deep-rooted feelings and desires.

✍ A tall, high house, with lots of stairs, spires or slanting roof shows aspirations and ideals. The shape of them will show you how you are progressing in obtaining these ideals.

✍ Was the front door big or small and easy to open? A large door means you are open to scrutiny from others, while a small door signifies someone who is more secretive.

Just as we all have an 'inner' child, we have an 'inner house' which reflects different aspects of our psyche. Each part of our outer home has an inner counterpart. If we pay attention to a particular element of our home it can affect the corresponding part of ourselves.

So how does our outer house connect to our inner house? Like our body, buildings are constructed on a basic foundation, have a framework or skeleton, are supplied with vital systems, have a varying number of stories and a host of special decorative features. Similarly, our psyche has a foundation which is set through genetic design and early childhood experiences. Our inner framework is built out of the tools which we develop, such as language, patterns of thought and learned responses. The vital systems of water, air and energy are like our body's respiratory, circulation and digestive systems. Our individual personality, skills and creativity are our inner house's special features, style and decoration, while the atmosphere of the house is our emotional and spiritual energy.

The upper stories of our inner house are those parts of our nature that link to other people and the world outside us. The lower levels of our inner house are those aspects of ourselves that are buried from view, and it is in the basement that we hide our deep-seated fears and anxieties.

The house can also represent the summary of our life. The basement and foundations are set in our early years and we add stories onto our house as we develop and mature.

The more complex we are and the more we learn and grow, the more intricate the shapes and design of our inner house will be.

To really come to know ourselves, we must first create a place of peace, calm and security, much like our own mother's womb. Our external home will then become a place where we can leave the world and listen to our own rhythms. This is why it is extraordinarily important that we create a place where we feel at ease with ourselves and once we cross the threshold we can shut the door and be at one.

One way to explore your inner house is through a creative visualization or meditation where you imagine a house which upon entering reflects who you are. Calm your mind and slow down your breathing. Let a picture of a house appear and know that it is your inner house. First look at the exterior of your house. What does it look like? Is it large or small, what shape is it? Does it have many doors and windows and what do they look like? When you are ready, walk through the front door and through your house noting the rooms, the number of stories, the colors, smells, furniture and any special features. When you have done this, draw your house or any aspect of it that is particularly significant to you and draw it with colored pens or pencils.

THE OPEN WINDOWS OF THIS HOUSE SYMBOLIZE OUR ABILITY TO INTERACT WITH THE OUTSIDE WORLD AND TO ASSIMILATE NEW IDEAS.

❧ Warm colors inside show an extrovert personality while cool colors a more introverted nature.

❧ Every object in your house strikes a deep chord within you and symbolizes an aspect of yourself. Was the furniture soft and comfortable or hard and bare? Did it have any association with another person and if it did, this may signify that you need to resolve some matter with that person.

❧ Consider now where in your house you are at the moment. If you feel that you are on the lower floors this shows you feel a need to rebuild some aspect of yourself. If you are on a higher level it is likely that you have a desire to grow and change. If you are on the roof, you will be filled with creative energy or showing a longing for spiritual growth.

Building Self-esteem

Our physical home can help us build self-esteem and enhance our sense of self. If we create a comfortable home, it will help us to be comfortable with ourselves.

When we look around at items that are meaningful to us, we reinforce our individuality and sense of self. Most of us fill our homes with an accumulation of things with which we have no particular connection. It is often only when we move house that we get around to sorting out the mountains of clutter. In fact, we will probably find only a dozen or so pieces that we really like and which accurately reflect our taste and character. It is these favorite items that may be things that we like to keep hidden so we can enjoy them in private.

Help or hindrance?

Write down some things you enjoy doing and an attitude or emotion you would like to promote, and discover whether your home is helping or hindering you in achieving these wishes. Homes naturally influence our lifestyle but can also help us realize our full potential. To create a home which can help us de-stress and enhance our quality of life, we need to look closely at the way we live.

Shaman healer Denise Linn tells us that 'when you change your outer reality, your inner reality can also change. You can dramatically alter the conditions of your life simply by implementing changes in the energy fields in your living environment.'

The way you structure your daily routine will influence your general well-being. If you create time and space for a good meal and exercise regularly, you will feel the overall benefits of a full and balanced life. Once you have an understanding of your current lifestyle you can create a home space where you can relax and be you.

Draw a circle and divide it into segments, each for an area of your life. Write in each segment the part of your life it represents. You may include such titles as work, relationship, home, garden, family, friends, hobby, charity work, spiritual development. If your circle is divided into work and relationship, you will see that when either one of these aspects is taken from you, you will only have the other left. This is why it is easy to become a workaholic if you have no relationship. If, however, your circle has many segments you will have a much fuller and more balanced life. Take away one aspect and you will still have the others to fill your time and attention.

Now draw another circle of the lifestyle you would like to have. Think about the proportions of time spent on the different areas of your life. Could you do more around the home? Could you spend more time creatively or relaxing? Once you have identified your ideal lifestyle, you will be able to change elements in your home to help you achieve this.

OUR SENSE OF IDENTITY CAN BE ENHANCED BY A BEDROOM THAT IS FILLED WITH SPECIAL BOOKS AND MEMENTOES.

Stress

HOW STRESSED ARE YOU?

Here are some questions you can ask yourself to assess whether you are suffering from stress: answer 'Yes' or 'No'

❧ Are you feeling disorganized and generally untidy?

❧ Are you having difficulty sleeping or in waking up?

❧ Do you often lose keys, glasses and other small items?

❧ Are you spending a great deal of time watching television or videos?

❧ Do you have any eating disorders or a weight problem?

❧ Do you have a desire to buy or collect things and bring them home?

❧ Do you lack a creative outlet or hobby?

❧ Are you feeling anti-social and dislike entertaining?

❧ Are you finding it difficult to exercise regularly?

As we live in an increasing state of social and environmental stress our general health and experience of life is largely dependent on our ability to handle the physical and emotional pressures we face. There are many ways we can learn to handle negative influences. First, we can avoid polluted areas and try not to work in situations that promote tension. We can also learn how to relax and try to lead a more healthy and balanced lifestyle.

Are you feeling disorganized and generally untidy?

Some homes are full of personal clutter and may be considered messy, but there is a difference between healthy and unhealthy clutter. Healthy clutter may be collections of personal items which reflect the personality and interests of the person who lives there. Their personal collections provide them with inspiration and give off comforting and supportive vibrations. The negative sort of clutter is that which reflects laziness and lack of self-love and may consist of things like dirty clothing, left-over food, unopened letters and general mess. This sort of clutter creates the feeling of dirtiness, irritability and generally hampers everyday life.

If you feel you have unhealthy clutter around you or feel a bit disorganized, clear up everything and sort things out. Give items away, especially if they are taking up space, or hold a garage sale.

Try to give your home a feeling of spaciousness, which may be difficult if it is filled with heavy or dark furniture. Light creamy yellow colors on walls or yellow and gold in furnishings would stimulate your mind and assist with clear thinking. Make sure you have ample storage cupboards, boxes, drawers and shelves, and that every item has a permanent home. If you are short of space, think laterally. Perhaps you could store things under the floor, in the roof space or create storage under a bed or above a door.

Are you having difficulty sleeping or in waking up?

One of the first effects of stress in our lives is restless sleep and insomnia. The healing home can be of wonderful assistance to you if you create a more tranquil and restful bedroom. A dark room promotes sleep, so curtains, blinds or drapes should be thick enough to cut out light completely.

Choose a bedroom in the house which is away from the road or noisy side of your property, even if it was previously used for another purpose. Ensure it is decorated in restful colors like pinks, peaches, soft blues and greens. These color vibrations all help with relaxation. A blue colored light bulb in your bedside light is calming and soothing (see page 105). Have the blue light on for half an hour before you go to sleep. You could also have a warm bath before you go to bed, using some essential oils that promote sleep. Do not have a television in your bedroom, as this only stimulates the brain, making it difficult for the mind to switch off.

If you find it difficult to wake up in the morning you may need to tune to your natural body cycles and nature's rhythms. It may be you are not motivated to rise and shine, and you need to have a reason to get up in the morning. Try having a routine or arrange a task which you have to do at a certain time. Go for a morning walk, take up yoga or Tai Ch'i, or have a household chore to perform. Check whether enough morning sunlight is entering your bedroom and if you have thick or dark-colored curtains, draw them to one side or add some sheer fabric behind them. These will allow you to wake up with the natural dawn.

Do you often lose keys, glasses and other small items?

Our moods and emotions can be greatly enhanced by the healing home. Small things that constantly irritate us can be eradicated by a little planning and organization. The best strategy is to make sure all small items have a home. Buy yourself an attractive key rack which can be placed on a wall near the front or back door. Alternatively, have a hall shelf, table or cupboard where you can put out a basket or bowl in which to place your keys and other items as soon as you come in. Glasses and pens can also disappear with amazing regularity. If you have reading glasses, get a small table with a drawer and place it next to your reading chair.

If you have a desk at home, make sure you have a glass, mug or container in which to place your pens or pencils. You can also buy pens with cords, similar to those used for glasses, to hang around your neck.

Are you spending a great deal of time watching television or videos?

We often fall in front of a television after a tiring day at work but watching too much television can also be a sign that you lack motivation for life. Television viewing can be relaxing if we choose the time and type of program we watch but many people's lives have become ruled by their viewing habits. Instead of having a recuperating effect, watching hours of television only adds to our stress and lack of vitality. Slumping in front of the box when tired allows our sub-conscious mind to take in impressions which we have to process at a later time. This usually happens at night, which is the only time left for the mind to assimilate and make sense of the day. So try not to have the television in the bedroom, especially if you do not sleep well.

Like road hogs, there are television hogs. If you like to watch television as a family, you need to position it in an area where there is enough comfortable seating for everyone. Remember that too much television can ruin conversation between family members. If you have arranged your seating around a television set, disguise it while it is not in use. Place an attractive screen in front of the set or throw over a cloth or rug. Your living room will look more attractive, and you will not be so tempted to turn on the set.

HOW STRESSED ARE YOU? (CONT)

✐ Are you feeling a need for space and privacy?

✐ Are you frustrated because you cannot put your ideas into practice?

✐ Are you suffering from an emotional crisis or extreme moodiness?

✐ Are you unable to concentrate on anything and dislike reading?

For each '**Yes**', score 1 point; for each '**No**', score 0 points. *Scores of between 1 and 5:* you appear to be coping well with your everyday life and are not displaying any significant signs of stress. Find ways to make your healing home enhance your sense of well-being. *Scores of between 5 and 7:* you are showing some signs of stress. Make use of your healing home to reduce stress levels before they get too great. *Scores of 8 and higher:* this signals a high stress factor and you are advised to introduce changes in your home to help you relax and build up your resistance.

If you do most of your viewing alone, find a place that is private and where you will not disturb other people in the house. This is especially so if the other members of the household enjoy listening to music, reading or pursuing some hobby.

Do you have any eating disorders or a weight problem?

For many people, their hurried lifestyle means that they spend less time preparing and eating their food. No wonder people who live on junk food and take little time to relax and enjoy a meal suffer more from stress. Meal time is a special time when we can unwind and enjoy being with our family or friends.

Preparing the dinner should be a creative and relaxing activity and a way to help you achieve this is by making the kitchen a friendly place to be. Surround yourself with bowls of fresh food and herbs. The colors and aromas will inspire and energize you. A cheerful vase of flowers can make the kitchen a less utilitarian place. Sip a glass of your favorite wine to help your creative, as well as your gastric, juices flow.

It is important that the cook should not work in isolation, so make sure the kitchen is a pleasant place for family and friends to gather and help with food preparation if necessary. If you can, have a table in the kitchen, or at least a couple of stools so you can eat or chat informally and if you are on your own, listen to the radio as it takes the loneliness out of the kitchen.

It is essential that we eat our meals sitting down, so that we receive the maximum nourishment from our food. By sitting at a table

we chew more slowly, and give time for our digestion to work properly. Eating at a table has many psychological benefits too. Read a newspaper or magazine, interact with others, look at a bowl of flowers or stare out of the window – these are all ways to calm the mind and soothe the emotions.

Do you have a desire to buy or collect things and bring them home?

Sorting and organizing gives us the feeling of control and security and this often turns people into collectors. If this natural desire to control our life and our environment becomes too strong it can turn into obsessive behavior, leading to shopping sprees or even kleptomania.

Half of the enjoyment of collecting is in the spotting, identifying and grouping like objects together. The things you can collect need not be expensive. In fact, the most unusual and rewarding collections are those that are found accidentally, or natural objects discovered on a walk in a park, forest or countryside. I collect pebbles and stones, and love picking things up on the beach near where I live.

Collecting objects can become a satisfying and interesting hobby. When you go out walking or shopping you have a focus which inspires you to learn more about the things you collect. It can also bring you into contact with other people with the same interest. Displaying your collection at home confirms who you are. Surrounding yourself with special things gives your life more meaning and purpose. So if you have a collection, don't pack it away in boxes in the garage, take pleasure in finding a place for it in your home.

EVERY OBJECT IN A COLLECTION HAS A HISTORY REMINDING US OF HAPPY OUTINGS AND SPECIAL FINDS.

MAKING SPACE

What we all need is a place and a time when we can make a mess and leave it there. If you don't have a spare room, garage, studio or workshop, create a place on a kitchen or side table. Spread out the tools and things you require for your hobby in the knowledge that you need not clear them away until you are finished. Sometimes you may need to work on a large area, like the living room floor. Choose a time when you know the room will not be used and let other members of the household know what you will be doing. Once you have made arrangements of time and space in your home you will find you have relieved yourself of most of the pressures and worries that have prevented you from your creative venture.

Do you lack a creative outlet or hobby?

I have met many people who wish they had a hobby while others suffer from a creative block. The reason for this is usually a result of their work, leaving little time or energy for relaxing pursuits.

Modern society has placed a stigma on sensual pleasures, especially touch. We are continually bombarded by the media on hygiene and cleanliness. Children are constantly told 'not to touch' or 'don't get your clothes dirty'. As a result, as adults we are very hesitant about getting our hands dirty with soil or paint. We have also been brainwashed into believing that our home should always be neat and tidy.

Our creativity is also hampered when the home is not supportive and there is lack of space. Having no play area at home means that we can feel restricted and less motivated to take up a relaxing pastime. Sometimes it is our attitude that prevents us picking up a paint brush or needle and thread, or taking up a hobby like photography.

Are you feeling anti-social and dislike entertaining?

Have you ever wondered why it is that you enjoy visiting some people at home more than others? You may visit people who are not your best friends but their social gatherings go on until late and everyone is reluctant to leave. Obviously the company is all important, but the subtle environment also plays an important role. The room's lighting and general ambiance of the home helps you to feel comfortable and relaxed, and a room with happy vibrations is much more welcoming than one which is filled with unhappiness.

Think carefully about the purpose of your entertainment and what you would like to offer your guests. It may be that you want to provide an informal atmosphere or you may not like people to linger too long.

It may be that you have to give formal dinner parties which are work-related. In this case, you may be more concerned about creating the right impression and so your living and dining areas reflect expected taste rather than your own. Take careful stock of your priorities, and decide who is more important, you or your occasional guests!

We are all becoming more relaxed about entertaining, and this can take the form of informal gatherings involving chatting, watching videos, playing a game or listening to music. Each of these activities can be enhanced by thoughtful planning of your home. Warm, rich colors can enhance the welcoming feeling your home creates. Style and placement of furniture also have a strong effect on your guests' behavior and comfort. For instance, if you wish to encourage conversation, make sure that your chairs or sofas are not too far apart. Having to shout across large, open spaces kills both private exchanges and a cozy atmosphere.

When you invite friends or family to your home, make a conscious decision to enjoy yourself, no matter how you are feeling. Your emotional vibrations and thoughts will permeate the atmosphere of the room and will influence you and your guests' enjoyment.

Are you finding it difficult to exercise regularly?

Our home environment works together with our lifestyle to either enhance or drain our energy levels. Regular exercise, eating a balanced diet and making relaxation time obviously increase our physical vitality, but living in a healthy, light and airy home will also raise the oxygen levels in the blood and help us avoid breathing in toxic pollutants in the air and water.

Our ability to relax also directly affects our energy levels. If we do not get quality sleep or know how to mentally relax we cannot set in motion our body's own healing and regenerative powers. Here the healing home environment plays a major role. Plan your home so that it is a relaxing place for you. Choose colors which you find soothing and which let you unwind. Make a place where you can catnap, have a massage or meditate. A patio or garden can also provide the ideal environment for relaxation activities.

The bathroom is a room which is often neglected. Try to create a room in which you wish to linger and pamper yourself (see also pages 92-9).

Are you feeling a need for space and privacy?

As our cities grow bigger and more densely populated, personal privacy is becoming a valuable commodity. Rather than linking us to the outside world, the home is becoming a sanctuary protecting us from the world.

Children also need privacy, a place where they can hide and feel safe and cozy. Parents might forget this, as children often share rooms until they are teenagers. Adults also require a room or place in the home where they can feel relaxed and private. In many homes, a few minutes in the bathroom is all the privacy that is available.

The most ideal situation is to have a room of your own. A study or sewing room. But if space is short, a special chair, window seat or table can provide a place where you can feel totally secure and withdraw from the world. Even when we go out we need privacy and often mark out an area for ourselves. A mother will often spread a blanket or towel on which her child can play or sleep. We also lay out a cloth when we go for a picnic or find a particular rock or tree on which to hang our belongings.

Are you frustrated because you cannot put your ideas into practice?

Many artists, writers, painters, healers and sensitive, creative people are prone to daydreaming and flights of fantasy. They find it hard to relate to everyday life and practical tasks and often their good ideas never take form. If you are one of these people, you can use your home environment to help you to become more practical and action-orientated.

If you are a person who lives mostly in your mind, you will require spiritual grounding and connection with the earth. The earth is the element which gives us motivation and stamina and literally 'brings us down to earth'. This element also draws us into our physical body, so that we can put our ideas and plans into action.

The color of the earth is red, and this includes all earthy colors like ochre, sienna, terracotta, peach and apricot, rusts and nutty browns. These colors will enhance your earth connection. Natural objects made of earth or clay can also be used for grounding. These stimulate your physical senses and pull you down out of your mind. Some people might

MULTI-PURPOSE SPACES

In cultures where living is a shared experience, gathering, sleeping and bathing spaces are separated by soft divisions. Hanging fabrics, blinds or screens are used to demarcate different areas in the home. There is a trend towards more shared living and many modern homes are perfect for introducing soft divisions. If you live in a building which allows you to create multi-purpose spaces, consider making an open-plan kitchen or creating a bedroom in an open loft space.

think this a bad thing, but earthy tones and furnishings provide you with strength and motivate you to follow your star.

Are you suffering from an emotional crisis or extreme moodiness?

The loving home can give you support and nourishment in difficult times. It can help you balance your emotions in many ways. For example, soothing and supporting colors have a calming effect on changing moods and emotions. Shades of pink, peach, apricot and warm tan give out love vibrations which help to heal the heart.

Flowers and aroma also emit strong healing vibrations. For the best effect, choose red, pink, lavender and white flowers. Walking past a bowl of scented flowers is immediately uplifting. Use aromatic oils in your bath and burn them in your home. Geranium balances the emotions, and frankincense or sandalwood have a stabilizing quality.

Surround yourself with plants, and try to spend time in a garden, park or even planting or re-potting indoor plants. The earth and nature has strong healing qualities. This is why we intuitively go for walks in a park or in the country when we need to balance and heal our emotions. Caring for a living thing, whether it is another person, animal or plant, helps focus our attention outside ourselves and build self-esteem and selfless love.

Display objects in your home that remind you of good times. Photographs of people who you love and love you bring comfort and aid the healing process. Always have pictures of yourself around you too, especially ones that are flattering and show you doing things you like.

Are you unable to concentrate on anything and dislike reading?

This may seem a strange question at first glance but books add a special dimension to a home. Collected within their pages are the experiences, thoughts and ideas of a great number of people, both living and dead. Books therefore contain unifying and bonding vibrations. In fact, a home without books remains a very cold and uninviting place. Colorful books and magazines contribute to the overall feeling in a room and book displays, in particular, create a very nourishing and friendly environment.

Unfortunately, fewer and fewer people are finding time to read. Magazines and newspapers are becoming more popular as reading material. So often with reading it is a case of out of sight, out of mind. Having reading matter accessible encourages you to pick up a book or paper and to spend time in a quiet relaxing way. If you find that your life is dull and lacks luster, reading can stimulate your imagination and encourage you to broaden your outlook.

If you don't know where to house your books, build shelves up a staircase or passageway. You can then pick up a reference book on your way downstairs to study or find a fiction title for a bedside read on your way up. Create a reading corner or nook. This can be a room within a room. Put a chair with a good reading light into a room, build in a window seat.

Use books and magazines as inspiration for your decorating ideas. Pick out ideas that suit your house style and your personal preferences. Make a scrapbook or file of these pictures and see whether you can identify a common thread or theme.

BOOKS LINING THE WALLS CAN TURN A WALK UPSTAIRS OR DOWN INTO AN INTERESTING EXPERIENCE.

The Power House

Many people are sensitive to the vibrations in buildings. When they enter a room they pick up the lingering atmosphere. Sometimes it is peaceful and calming and at other times, sorrowful or uncomfortable.

Every building absorbs and holds vibrations in its walls, floors and furnishings. The older the building, the more layers of energy have been stored while a new building probably only contains the vibrations of the workmen who built it. Strong emotions like anger and hate can remain for a long time, especially when a room has been unused or closed up for a period of time. Negative vibrations can linger for hundreds of years before being released, which is why old buildings contain so much atmosphere.

When you move into a new apartment or house, it is most important to clear the energy in it. Negative vibrations in your existing home should also be cleansed after a quarrel or when someone you dislike has entered. You should also clear your home of toxic fumes and positive ions which build up from time to time.

Toxic vibrations in the home can be caused by both internal and external forces. The first is caused by negative vibrations left by people who have been there. The second relates to the building itself as well as the furniture, furnishings and equipment in it. The third relates to outside conditions and especially energy coming from the ground under the house. Once you have cleared the energy using any one or combination of the ways shown in this chapter, you can then enhance the energy in your home by instilling positive vibrations using air, sound, aroma and color.

EVERY ROOM HAS A PARTICULAR ATMOSPHERE CREATED BY THE VIBRATIONS HELD IN THE
FLOOR, WALLS AND FURNISHINGS.

Vibrations from the Past

Every house has a history. The signs which indicate its age and development over the years are preserved within its structure and interior furnishings, while documents can give the legal history and information about the people who lived there or once owned the property. Even the site where a modern house has been built will have its history, which is every bit as interesting as that of an older building.

There will be many clues on your doorstep regarding the history of your home such as in the names of the house, street, neighborhood. There will also be oral traditions relating to the area and photographs, magazines and books on local history.

Information about the past owners of the house may come from your neighbors or, if they have changed recently, can be found in documents relating to the title deeds. There may also be other documents that reveal details about the house which were not intended as records to be used for that purpose, such as newspaper articles, wills or photographs. Looking at a map will also help you find out more about the site of your house in its context over the years.

Often old buildings hold vibrations of the previous occupants and sometimes from those that have lived there a long time ago. In houses where there are lots of corners and ornaments, unusual shaped rooms and hidden spaces, energy can remain trapped. A room that has thick, old-fashioned wallpaper, old carpeting and draped curtains is also prone to holding energy from previous occupants. This is why there are so many tales of ghosts associated with old houses with such heavy furnishings. We can also use our sensitivity to access the psychic atmosphere.

The previous inhabitants of your house also leave their energetic mark. If they enjoyed a generally happy and healthy life there, they will have instilled positive vibrations into the building. If possible, try to find out about the previous occupants of your home in the ways I have suggested. Even if the vibrations in your home feel good, you can still give them a spring clean in case some stagnant energy remains. This suggestion is based on a clearing ritual suggested by Shaman healer Denise Linn.

First, starting from the door, walk around the room in a clockwise direction. Clap you hands loudly and rhythmically, forming circles in the air. When you reach a corner in the room clap your hands several times in an upwards motion. As you progress around the room, listen to the sound of your clapping and try to locate any spots where the sound is dull. Now go back to these areas and clap your hands in sweeping movements towards the nearest window. Check the sound of your clapping again. It should be crisp and clear.

Family heirlooms

Furniture in a house tells the story of the humans who live there. Few things are as satisfying as seeing yourself reflected in your

personal possessions. We become attached to objects for the associations and memories they hold for us. So long-possessed and cherished furniture exudes a warmth coming from its beauty and the affection felt for it.

Family heirlooms often hold the key to many generations of owners. The energy held in this furniture can influence the well-being of the present owners. If you are in tune with your ancestors, and honor and respect the piece of furniture, it can become a guardian and defender of the home.

Furniture can remind you of people, special times in your lives and other places. If you chose a piece of furniture when you were struggling financially, getting married, getting divorced or moving home, you will recall these times when you look at or use the item. This means that you are constantly and very subtly reminded of these connections. If the furniture was an unwanted gift or you do not like it, it will continue to reinforce these feelings of discomfort, anger, or resentment.

Get rid of any unwanted furniture. If you do not, it will undermine your self-esteem and happiness, lowering the energy field of your entire home. If you cannot do this, disguise the furniture by re-covering, using mounds of cushions or throwing a tablecloth over the top. This will not get rid of the vibrations but will deflect them elsewhere.

ONLY KEEP FURNITURE YOU REALLY LIKE.

A FAMILY HEIRLOOM CAN BECOME A GUARDIAN AND DEFENDER OF THE HOME.

Clearing Strong Emotions

WHEN TO CLEANSE

☞ When you move house.

☞ After an argument or quarrel.

☞ After an unwelcome visitor has called.

☞ When you have expressed anger, hate, jealousy.

☞ When you are depressed or despairing.

☞ After illness.

☞ After a violent or distressing television program.

☞ After a loud noise, for example made by neighbors or builders.

☞ After a smoker has been in the room.

☞ If someone has died in the house.

We don't just look at our surroundings, we experience them with all our senses. We drink in the sounds, scents and tactile sensations around us. Many places deny us these sensory perceptions. A dead and sterile environment is therefore a form of sensory deprivation and our home could induce us to feel cold and isolated.

If we are able to let our emotions flow freely outwards, we usually do this in the privacy of our home. There are many occasions when other people express their emotions in our home too. Once we relieve ourselves of these pent-up feelings we usually feel a great deal better, but we forget that we have sent out vibrational waves into the air around us. Our homes collect all these vibrations, good and bad, and reflect them back to us at some time. So it is very important that we clear these negative energy patterns.

To do this, play some music which you enjoy. Music that instills the room with love can lift and transform any harmful emotional energy. Fill the room with this music and concentrate on filling it with the power of love. Buy a bunch of deep pink or white roses. These will emit love vibrations through their aroma and color. Different roses will send out different kinds of love rays.

Unwelcome visitors

There are many occasions when we have unwelcome visitors in our home, causing us to become anxious and on guard. We can use our healing home to help us on these occasions. In a protected home, these people do not stay for long. If you have filled your home with happy thoughts and love vibrations, it is not unusual for the unwanted guest to pick these up and become calm and more peaceful. If they were bringing you bad news or came to confront you in an argumentative fashion, the loving vibrations will disarm them. You will then be able to deal with the situation in a more peaceful and calm way.

Once they have left, it is best to clear the space where they have been. If they have been sitting in a chair, run your hands over it several times, drawing up the negative energy and sweeping it away. You can direct the energy towards the light or if this is not possible towards a plant which will absorb the negative energy and transform it into light.

Now sit quietly in the chair you have cleared. Close your eyes and focus on your breathing until you feel calm and still. Slowly let a picture form of this person walking towards you with arms outstretched and with a gentle smile. See the person stop a little way from you and greet you. You feel very calm and peaceful. Now say, 'Thank you for the lessons you have taught me. Go in peace.' Watch the person turn around and walk away.

Meditate in the room until you feel calm. Then send out calming thoughts to the room. Pray for assistance in clearing harmful and impure vibrations from the room. Ask that, 'all that is harmful, negative and impure leave this room and be transformed into light.'

The Toxic Home

The second type of harmful vibrations which can fill your home are caused by chemicals and pollutants emitted from the materials used to build the structure of your home and those given off by materials used inside. If these vibrations are not allowed to escape through natural ventilation and the fabric of the walls and ceiling, they can have a serious effect on your health.

Sick building syndrome has been carefully documented and bad environmental conditions can cause such ailments as asthma, sinusitis, headaches, eye strain, skin irritations, lung problems, neck and back pain, nausea, tiredness and even fits. Just as serious is the psychological impact of sick building syndrome on its occupants. Loss of concentration, low motivation, a critical outlook and depression are just some of the effects of living in such a building.

If you or your family are suffering from any of these ailments it is likely that your home may be contributing to your problems. Try to remember when the symptoms first occurred and check whether you had made any changes to your home at around the same time. In one case it was discovered that several people started to feel dizzy and nauseous just after they had purchased a microwave oven. The oven was tested and found to be ill-fitted so was leaking radiation into the kitchen.

To discover possible sources of toxic vibrations in your home, make a checklist of the building. You first need to check external factors such as ground, air and sound pollution. Then check the building itself, starting from the floor upwards. The text over the next few pages provides you with some ideas of areas to look closely at when checking the toxicity of your home.

Cellars, garages, services

Oil tanks can leak vapors and integral garages can also create fumes which can permeate the whole house. Ideally, garages should be separate from the main house, but if this is not possible keep any doors and windows shut while warming up your car. Also make sure you keep your garage door open long enough to let out any exhaust fumes.

Look at the services coming into the building and check that there are no leaks or faulty joins. Lead pipes can poison the water as can soldered copper pipes. Metal paints can give off toxic fumes, so use natural paints for pipes, and plastic ones above ground.

Floorcoverings

Look at the types of floorcoverings in your home. Wooden boards can give off resin vapors so it is best to use old or recycled wood and seal boards with a natural varnish or sealant. Vinyl and plastic floorcoverings also emit vinyl chloride vapors and are environmentally harmful. Use linoleum which is a natural product, or stone or ceramic tiles, all of which are hardwearing and can be easily

cleaned. Naturally sealed cork is a good floor-covering where warmth is needed.

If you have carpeting, make sure it is made from a natural material like wool, hessian, seagrass or coir. Nylon and polyester carpets give off vapors and insecticides which we breathe in. The adhesive used in underlay can also give off vapors, so use a natural underlay made of cotton, hessian or linen.

Walls, paints and varnishes

If you are doing any internal alterations, make sure you use natural gypsum plaster-board and lime plaster. Both plaster and cement give off formaldehyde and radon which can be most harmful. Also check for any asbestos insulation as the fibers and dust can be highly toxic. If you do find any in your walls or ceiling, call in an expert to remove it.

All building materials, such as bricks, aggregate blocks, concrete and stone, have the potential to be contaminated with radium and radon, depending on the location of source. The best way to check for the prescence of these is by dowsing with a pendulum (see page 48).

The walls of our home are its skin, through which it must breathe and eliminate any toxins to the outer surface. It cannot do this if non-porous paints have been used, and all the harmful vibrations are trapped within. Consequently, it is essential to use natural non-toxic paint when decorating. These are now widely available in an array of beautiful colors. Remember that paints, varnishes and stains give off toxic vapors, especially while drying, so make sure of good ventilation while the paint dries.

Heating and kitchen appliances

The fuels we use for heating and cooking can be exceedingly dangerous if levels of harmful by-products cannot escape from the home. If your home is well sealed, has little ventilation, non-porous paints and building materials, it can trap these toxic fumes.

Gas-heaters and water heaters can easily leak from pilot lights and produce toxic fumes. Check that these systems are vented well to the outside and serviced regularly.

Another common source of carbon monoxide fumes are those escaping from chimneys when wood or coal is burned. Get your chimney cleaned regularly and, if possible, install a sealed primary or secondary combustion stove which is both attractive, safe and environmentally friendly.

Gas cookers can also produce lethal amounts of carbon monoxide. They emit other harmful gases, too, such as carbon dioxide and sulphur dioxide, reducing our ability to absorb oxygen causing headaches, dizziness, nausea, loss of appetite and adversely affecting our respiratory system.

Refrigerators are the biggest contributors to chlorinated fluorocarbons (CFCs) which cause the breakdown of the delicate ozone layer around the earth. If you cannot afford a new low CFC model, try to use a smaller refrigerator and create a larder to keep your food fresh and cool.

Furniture and furnishings

For many years foam filling was used in chairs, cushions, pillows and mattresses until

NATURAL FABRICS USED IN A ROOM WITHOUT TELEVISION CREATES A HEALTHIER ATMOSPHERE AND A PLACE WHERE YOU CAN RELAX.

it was realized what a serious fire hazard polyurethane presented. There are now many safer and more healthy alternatives.

Fabrics, too, can be hazardous if they have been treated with chemicals. Many have been colored with synthetic dye-stuff and the by-products of the process contribute to ground and river pollution. Always check the labels of garments before purchasing and try to find unbleached fibers.

Household products

Many household cleaners such as polish, bleach and detergent are both toxic and irritants. Aerosol sprays also emit chlorinated fluorocarbons. Get into the habit of using natural products and home remedies. Buy products with natural pump action sprays. Many of these are reusable and it is not difficult to make your own air fresheners and household sprays (see pages 88-9).

Electrical equipment

Electrical equipment in the home such as televisions, radios, computers, microwaves, dish washers and other appliances can fill your home with harmful energy. Not only do these items expose us to radiation and harmful electrical charges, but the energy they consume has a detrimental effect on our natural environment.

There is a growing awareness that electric blankets can interfere with your body's natural electrical field. Exposure to electrical currents in this way can trigger allergies and cause various problems like high blood pressure and disturbed sleep patterns.

Energy Conservation

SAVING ENERGY IN YOUR KITCHEN

☞ Do not use your washing machines for half washes. Wait until you have a full load.

☞ Wash your dishes by hand.

☞ Cook several things in your oven at one time.

☞ Use a saucepan wider than the ring and cover the pan with a lid.

☞ Use heavy-based cookware to help distribute the heat efficiently.

☞ Use a pressure cooker to reduce cooking time.

☞ Purchase food more often instead of using a deep freeze.

☞ Cut down on kitchen gadgets that use energy; many of them take longer to assemble and clean than the job would have taken by hand.

Well-designed homes are cheaper to maintain than houses that need expensive, energy-consuming heaters, air conditioners, humidifiers or ionizers. The healing home allows people to live in warmth and comfort without recourse to oil-based fuels. It is no longer sensible to buy a house that does not save energy or generates its own.

There are many ways to conserve energy in your home, and some of the ideas listed opposite are suggested by Bill Mollison in his book *The Introduction to Permaculture* in which he describes a workable design system for creating an ecologically sound and viable environment. Permaculture is based on the wisdom of ancient natural systems, and modern scientific knowledge. It uses the inherent qualities of plants and animals combined with the natural elements in the landscape to produce a life-supporting system in as small a space as possible.

Making your home radiant

To counteract these toxic and harmful vibrations, introduce forms of radiant energy through light, air, aroma and sound.
.

Light

Pure sunlight has a very powerful cleaning action. The light rays purify and cleanse all natural objects as well as any dark spiritual forces. Curtains and blinds hold dust and dirt particles as well as block out a good deal of natural light, so if you want to thoroughly cleanse a room it is a good idea to start by taking these down. The extra natural sunlight which will enter the room through the larger window area, will help clean the room while the curtains are being washed.

Wash the curtains and soft furnishings in a non-biological and bio-degradable washing powder or shampoo. You can add a few drops of essential oil to the rinsing water to add a refreshing smell to the fabrics. Lemon and citrus oils work very well. If there is any furniture remaining, make sure you clean it thoroughly with a natural upholstery or fabric cleaner.

If you wish to clear a room without removing any of the curtains or furnishings install a violet or purple light bulb, available in specialist light shops or from a color therapy studio. Place the bulb in the light socket in the room you wish to clear, and leave it on for one to two hours. Do not remain in the room while the light is on, as the colored light may be too powerful for you.

Air

Every house should be able to breathe. Just as natural fibers allow our skin to breathe, so does the home need to transport and eliminate bad odors, stale air and negative vibrations to the surface. It can do this by the use of porous natural materials like wood, clay brick, lime mortar and plaster, thatch, and porous non-toxic paints. This allows air and moisture to pass very slowly through the building by diffusion from inside to outside.

This process acts as a sieve, filtering out dust and moisture and it reduces pollutants. Choosing a house made from natural materials, or one which can be adapted to use them, will improve the energy field in your home.

To be healthy you need to breathe clean air. You also need to breathe deeply and properly so that you extract the maximum amount of oxygen and life-force energy from the air. Posture is a very important factor in breathing, and sitting hunched over a desk or table, and badly designed beds and chairs all contribute to our inability to breathe correctly.

Even if the air quality is bad out of doors you cannot assume it is better indoors. Household chemicals, fabrics and furnishings can give off chemical pollutants. Also dust and bacteria build up, creating a breeding ground for many ailments including asthma, hayfever, rashes, and susceptibility to colds and flu. Instead of sealing all available windows and doors, air a room if you wish to build up your resistance to viral infections.

The best way of clearing stale energy is to give the place a spring clean. Open the windows, checking any problems which need to be fixed. Leave the front and the back doors open so that you create a through-draft for half an hour. This will help flush out negative vibrations that may be clinging to the corners and ceilings. To create good cross-ventilation, open doors and windows on opposite walls and ends of the building. This will create pressure which will draw air through the home. Any moist air which is trapped in the

SAVING ENERGY IN YOUR HOME

Draft-proof all doors and windows. Sealing all cracks prevents heat leaking from the house or cold air entering.

Incorporate secondary glazing. This is not as costly as double glazing.

Open secondary- and double-glazed windows to provide good ventilation in the summer months, and to clear stale air from a room. Try to stick to wooden windows made from managed forests. These are more attractive and environmentally friendly.

If possible, attach a greenhouse to the sun-side. Even a window greenhouse or skylight are improvements as they bring in sunlight and will encourage plant growth. In cold areas, the greenhouse must be closed off from the rest of the house except for a high-level vent.

Add heat mass such as concrete slabs, tanks, and brick or stonework within the greenhouse or insulated warm rooms. These absorb and retain heat which is released at night.

Place a solar water heater on the roof to reduce or eliminate fuel-powered water heaters. Remember, you do not have to have direct sunshine, natural sunlight works as well. Solar panels are expensive, but will prove cost-effective if you intend remaining in this house for a few years.

Use vegetation to improve the microclimate, which is the particular climate around your home. Plant trees in a shape that will trap the sun, attach a trellis or plant shrubbery to the shady side of your house and place a windbreak of trees on the windy side.

Check that your doors and windows fit snugly.

Clean your chimney and get your boiler serviced regularly.

Turn off lights in rooms which you are not using.

Put tin foil behind electric radiators.

Only watch television programs that you like. Turn off the television at other times.

Alternate showering with bathing.

Use a hot water bottle and brushed cotton sheets instead of an electric blanket.

Dry your hair naturally when you can.

bathroom or kitchen can escape, so helping avoid dampness which breeds mold, fungi, bacteria and viruses.

Give the place a good dusting and clean the doors and woodwork with a safe non-toxic cleaning material like herbal soap, herbal cleaner and natural floor polish.

Remove anything which may produce toxic smells, such as plastic, rubber-backed or synthetic carpets, or a defective gas cooker. If you are not sure of the source of a bad odor, follow your nose! Even the places that look clean are likely to harbor dust and micro-organisms which carry bacteria, so clean out all your cupboards. Bicarbonate of soda will help remove any unpleasant smells from refrigerators and stoves.

Aroma

Burning aromatic oils in a room is an excellent way of clearing out unwanted vibrations, especially psychic forces. Aromas are vibrations which travel in the ether and, like color and sound, affect anything with which they come into contact. Our sense of smell is one of the oldest senses and it is one that we have almost lost, but associations with scent last longer than those from our other senses.

Different essential oils have different properties and actions upon us and our environment. Essential oil of juniper, lavender and frankincense have high vibrations. Tea tree essential oil, which has been used by the Aborigines in Australia for centuries, is a disinfectant as it has anti-bacterial and anti-fungal qualities. You can easily mix two or three of these oils together. If you are unable to obtain essential oils or burn them, buy some incense or joss sticks (see pages 86-7).

Sound

Sound vibrations are very powerful as they set up a resonance which can alter physical and etheric matter. Toning or humming sets up a pattern of wavelengths that can move any build-up of stagnant energy in a room. If you have never tried toning, start by making the A-U-M sound, letting the resonance build up in the base of the throat. Repeat this slowly and rhythmically for five minutes. This method works especially well when several people do it together.

If you have the equipment handy, it is also possible to play a tape or record to clear a room. Sadly, it has been shown that compact discs lack certain vibrations found in vinyl and tape recordings. These good sound vibrations are similar to the alpha waves produced by our brain during restful sleep. All forms of chanting disperse negative energy, so a tape of a Gregorian chant or Buddhist mantra will have a similar effect.

Cymbals, bells and gongs are good tools for moving energy. When you use them, do check that the neighbors won't be alarmed or disturbed.

Balancing energy

Good health, which is the basis of a long and happy life, is a state of energy balance. Energy in its undifferentiated state or potential is known by the Chinese as Tao. Tao is manifest in all things through the dynamic interaction of the two polar energy forces, yin and yang. There is no absolute yin or yang, just as there is no absolute light or darkness. Each exists relative to the other and are found in varying proportions in all things. This dynamic force

of energy constantly circulates within us and is a necessary condition of life.

There are also five basic types of energy that are found in varying proportions in all substances and phenomena. These are fire, water, earth, metal and wood. Fire is the most yang, while water is the most yin. The elements are identified with a specific body organ, color, planet, season and compass direction. Each element can either be creative or destructive, and each one of the five elements either feeds or destroys another.

In the creative cycle, fire creates earth as the ashes created by the fire return to the earth. The earth creates metal which is formed within it. Metal creates water through a process of condensation and water creates wood by nourishing plant and tree life, and finally wood fuels fire.

In the destructive cycle, fire destroys metal, metal destroys wood, wood destroys earth, earth destroys water and water destroys fire.

To maintain a balance of energy in your home, the five elements should work in harmony. When all these elements are present and working together, they will promote a happy, healthy home. Check that you have all elements present in your home. If you have too much of one element and not enough of another this can lead to inharmonious vibrations, so make sure you have similar proportions of each element or their related color. If you are lacking in any one element, add an appropriate object or its related color. For example, if you have no water element in your living room, you could add a blue or black object instead, while a bathroom with no fire element would benefit from some red or orange candles.

THE FIVE ELEMENTS

Metal
Related color: white
Introduce as: metal window frames, metal furniture, metal candlesticks, metal wind chime.

Water
Related colors: black or blue
Introduce as: pond, fountain, water feature, fish tank, bowl, vase of water.

Wood
Related color: green Introduce as: wooden windows, doors, floors, wood or bamboo furniture, paper screen.

Fire
Related color: red
Introduce as: candles, burning aromatic oils or incense.

Earth
Related color: yellow
Introduce as: clay bricks, clay tiles, ceramic crockery and containers, crystals.

CANDLELIGHT IS A SIMPLE WAY OF INTRODUCING YANG ENERGY TO HARMONIZE A COLD, DARK OR DAMP ROOM.

The Energetic Home

We have discovered that both occupants and buildings can produce negative energy in the home, but often these harmful vibrations can originate outside the home and especially from the earth over which it is built.

Divining and dowsing have been used successfully to locate energy disturbances and underground water for centuries. The earth has its own magnetic field, the north pole being the center of a negative electrical force, while the south pole is the center of the positive force. The whole earth is permeated by magnetic lines of energy which criss-cross over its surface in much the same way as a hair net. These lines are similar to our nervous system along which travels natural radiation, or the electromagnetic field (EMF). The natural radiation from the earth is very beneficial to us, and our connection to its energy helps us live in harmony with the earth and its rhythms.

In some places, these energy zones are particularly strong, and it is these places that have powerful healing properties. It may be water from a certain spring, or a mountain, hill or ancient mound which marks the area. Many standing stones were erected at points where lay-lines crossed and some places with this strong earth energy are regarded as fertility sites. You may be lucky enough to have your home over one of these healing sites.

When the natural EMF in the ground is disturbed, energy can become distorted. This is known as geopathic stress. This stress can be caused by natural phenomena such as underground faults and streams, but it can also be man-made. High-voltage power lines and electric cables, electrical appliances and synthetic materials can all cause geopathic stress. Many illnesses can be traced back to disturbances in ground radiation, and many more problems than we are presently aware of have their origins in these energy disturbances. The earth vibrations have been found to be the strongest at full moon and homes built over an area of magnetic stress expand and contract at this time.

AN OLD CLOCK CAN HARMONIZE OUR BODY RHYTHMS, WHILE SOFT NATURAL LIGHTING ENCOURAGES RESTFUL SLEEP.

Geopathic Stress

In the home, geopathic stress can affect your health, especially if you are sleeping over an underground stream or watercourse. This will affect your chest and lungs, and you will probably be susceptible to coughs, bronchitis, pleurisy and asthma. You will also feel cold at night and suffer from general tiredness and loss of energy in the day.

Places disturbed by negative energies can be very disruptive to sleep. If you sleep near high-voltage power lines or even over domestic supply cables, you will find that your sleep may be restless. If you find that your sleepless nights have no apparent reason, you may do well to check for underground disturbances. In severe cases, links have been found between illnesses such as cancer and leukemia and overhead power lines. Even electrical disturbances from electrical equipment in the bedroom can increase the risk of disease. These include seemingly harmless things like a radio, an alarm clock, bedside lights, television, iron and steel bed frames and sprung mattresses. Steel lintels and beams in the floor or ceiling can also distort the natural electromagnetic field.

There are three ways of checking the magnetic field in a room in your home, outlined below and opposite.

Using a dowsing rod

The rod used for dowsing can be a simple forked tree branch. Choose a rod which is approximately the thickness of a pencil and about 50 cm (18 in) long. The best rods are made from willow, witch-hazel or young maple, but any sapling wood will do as long as the rod is pliable and not likely to snap. When you have cut your rod, remove any small protruding twigs so that you have a smooth fork much like a chicken 'wish bone'.

Hold the forks of the rod in each hand with your palm facing upwards. Bring your elbows in to your sides so that you rest your clenched fists on your hips. Swing the rod end up so that it is slightly higher than your fists. When you reach an area of disturbance, the rod will gradually bend from the horizontal position, downward. Some dowsers find that the rod goes up instead of down.

Using a pendulum

A pendulum consists of a weight on a short length of string or chain. You can buy a crystal pendulum from a good complementary health shop, or you can make your own. The best pendulums are made using a natural quartz crystal as the weight. You will need to stick it onto a pendant clasp or ring so that you can thread a string or chain through it which should be not more than 6 in (15 cm) long. It is not advisable to use nylon thread or any thread which is stiff as this will interfere with the swing of the pendulum. You can also use buttons or wooden, ceramic or glass beads as a pendulum weight.

Before you can use a pendulum you need to discover what shape and direction is its normal swing. The pendulum will react differently for different people, but once you have found the direction of swing for yourself, this will remain constant. The pendulum has no magical power, it links directly to the unconscious mind of the user. This means that to use it successfully you will need to ask it very clear questions, so that your conscious mind does not interfere with the transference of energy from your higher mind to the pendulum. It is important that you do not use a pendulum when you are tired or emotionally stressed as the electromagnetic disturbance caused can interfere with the results.

Using a compass

Use a good compass. Turn it until the needle lies directly north and move it slowly over the area to be dowsed. As the compass approaches an area of disturbance, the needle will swing away from the north position. As it is difficult to hold a compass steady, it is best used over a small area like a bed, chair or sofa. Pass the compass over the area a number of times from different directions to ensure accuracy when pinpointing a disturbance.

Finding geopathic stress

To dowse for energy disturbances in the home, draw a plan of each room. This does not have to be exact, but it is best to pace out the rooms, so that you can pinpoint the spot where any disturbance may occur. If your room is six paces by five, draw a rectangle on squared paper, using one square per pace.

You will need to make a number of passes across the room or area in two directions which are at right angles to one another so that you are forming a grid. Then walk diagonally across the space.

Select a wall and start at the left-hand corner. Walk along the edge of the room slowly and steadily holding the compass. Count your paces as you move. If the compass moves from the north position, mark the spot on your plan. Depending on the size of the room, move two paces to the right and walk across the room again, marking any points where the compass moves off true north. Once you have walked across the room in several straight lines, move to an adjacent wall and start again. You will be forming a grid. When you have completed this grid you can walk diagonally from corner to corner in the same way.

Double check any points where you may have found disturbance. If they are small, mark them in blue on your plan, but if they are major disturbances mark them in red.

It may be that the metal frame in the furniture itself is the cause of the disturbance so check the bed, chair or sofa again, passing the compass carefully over it.

Use a pendulum in the same way, moving it slowly over the surface, and note any sudden or large changes in direction or the size of its swing. Use the grid system to check in both directions.

USING A PENDULUM

≈ Hold the pendulum over the floor or piece of furniture and ask it the following questions:

≈ Which direction indicates normal ground energy?

≈ Which direction indicates a disturbance in the energy pattern?

≈ Which direction indicates 'yes'?

≈ Which direction indicates 'no'?

≈ Note the results. A larger arc will indicate the presence of either positive or negative energy, depending on the direction of the swing.

The Lucky Home

Feng shui may be described as a subtle form of interior design and literally means 'wind and water'. The Chinese believe that these elemental forces shape our landscape and also have the power to affect our everyday life. They can affect our physical needs, mental well-being and financial security as well as harness the greater cosmic forces which govern the Universe. Major organizations all over the world have allocated funds so that feng shui masters will come to check the feng shui of their buildings.

In China, feng shui is a way of life and no decision is taken without referring to the vital force, or 'ch'i', which flows through the universe and can affect a person's health, wealth and happiness. To achieve harmony only requires that we honor and go with the flow of ch'i: living in harmony with nature and not by trying to conquer it.

By using the principles of feng shui it is possible to change any environment into one that supports us, one which will improve our relationships, our finances, our family relationships, health and career.

Where ch'i is blocked we should enhance its energy and where there are negative influences we can deflect these using a number of devices such as mirrors and wind chimes, which need to be carefully positioned. To create good feng shui, you need to identify the site and position of your home, as well as its shape, materials used and arrangement of your furniture.

We can all connect to the power of ch'i through our intuition, our common sense or by learning some practical principles which anyone can follow. For instance, it is bad feng shui if a tree has been planted too close to the building which may disturb the foundations. Living at the bottom of a hill, will mean there may be the possibility of flooding and this is also bad feng shui. On the other hand, if your house is built half-way up a hillside with an open view, the pleasing and uplifting effect will mean it is good feng shui.

THE OPEN VIEW OVER WATER GIVES THIS HOUSE GOOD FENG SHUI IN WHICH THE OCCUPANTS ARE LIKELY TO PROSPER.

Lucky Moves

THE BEST SITES FOR ROOMS IN THE NORTHERN HEMISPHERE

Reverse these directions for the southern hemisphere.

Sitting room South facing for late morning and afternoon sun.

Kitchen Southwest facing for morning and afternoon sun.

Dining room East or west facing for morning or afternoon sun.

Playroom West facing for afternoon sun.

Bedroom Southeast facing for morning sun.

Bathroom Any direction which allows the most light.

Study West or northwest facing for reflected light.

Storage/garage West or north facing for late afternoon sun.

Studio/office North facing for reflected light.

Exercise space East facing for morning sun or west facing for afternoon sun.

Meditation or sanctuary East facing for sunrise or west facing for sunset.

Even though a new home may be very appealing to us, its feng shui may hold a very different scenario. This can be illustrated by the great writer Rudyard Kipling who lived at Rock House on the East Devon coast at the turn of the last century. He describes the house as 'being almost too good to be true ... with big rooms each and all open to the sun.' Although this house at first appeared to be the perfect home it had a depressing effect on Rudyard. He writes, 'a gathering blandness of mind and sorrow of heart – caused by the Feng-Shui – the spirit of the house itself – a spirit of deep, deep despondency.'

A house can therefore be lucky or unlucky, so when choosing a place to live or when looking at your present home you need to assess the flow of ch'i through the building. This will help you decide whether the place is lucky or whether you need to correct the bad influences. To do this you need first to look at the site in relation to other buildings and features of the land and environment.

Ch'i energy consists of both yin and yang forces (see page 44). These are the two opposite and complementary forces in the Universe. Yin is the feminine force, while yang is masculine. They need to be in balance for harmony to reign and the best site for a house is where there is the most ch'i, a balanced meeting point of yin and yang energy.

Mountains and other raised features in the land are yang in nature and are thought to symbolize protective dragons. Rivers and streams are their veins through which passes the ch'i, or 'dragon's breath'. The shapes of the landscape reveal what type of dragon energy is present. A mountain which is shaped like an armchair is ruled by the protective Mountain dragon. A hill to the east of the mountain is ruled by the Green dragon while the White tiger rules a western hill. These two great creatures are like guards and must coordinate with one another.

Water, on the other hand, is very yin and ruled by the Water dragon. Water symbolizes wealth and the position of your house in relation to water will be of utmost importance.

The ideal position for a house

The most auspicious place for a house is halfway up a hillside, facing south, with the higher mountain to the rear. To the west should be a small hill and to the east a slightly higher hill. The front of the house should have an open and commanding view over a smaller foothill. Clean, gently moving, water in the form of a pond, lake or river should run in front of the house.

You can apply this principle to an urban situation. Taller buildings or trees should be at the back as they will form a protective guard for your house. It is best to have a building of similar size to the left and a slightly taller one on the right.

THE ELEMENTS OF WOOD AND FIRE ENHANCE EACH OTHER WHILE A LARGE MIRROR REFLECTS CH'I ENERGY INTO OTHER PARTS OF THE ROOM.

Feng Shui in the Home

GOOD EXTERNAL FENG SHUI

✍ The left- and right-hand side of the house is balanced without an extension to one side.

✍ The depth is greater than the width.

✍ A house that is the same height or higher than those opposite.

✍ A square back and round front, eg bay windows.

✍ The front of the house is at a lower level than the back.

✍ High land at the back.

✍ A back garden that is larger and wider than the front.

✍ A house that is built close to others and in a similar style.

✍ Lamp posts in the garden, but not in front of the door.

One of the most important parts of your home is the front door. This is the gateway into your private sanctuary and 'the mouth of ch'i'. The main door should be in scale with the building: it should not be too big or too small. The frame should be strong and straight and the door should fit well. If your door or frame is weak it will weaken the energy levels in your home and ch'i will escape through any cracks. The best location for the front door or your home is towards the left-side of the house as this is the 'knowledge' position of the house. It is also useful to have your garden enclosed by a wall to hold in the ch'i and aid further protection for the occupants. It is better if the walls are more than 2 yd (2 m) from the house.

Internally, do not clutter the rooms with furniture. This allows the energy and you to move freely around the house. Keep most of your decorations like pictures and ornaments hanging on the walls, which should be painted light colors.

The arrangement of furniture in your home is also significant and you can generally follow the rule that the home owner's chair, desk or table should have a commanding view of the door. In the living room, the wealth point is located at the top left-hand corner as you enter. If you are suffering from financial worries, place a large, round-leafed plant in this position in the room. A sofa should never be placed under a beam as this puts pressure on whoever is supporting the family. If a bed is placed under a beam it will have a negative effect on that person's health. Where the beam crosses the body will indicate which part of their health it will affect.

In the bedroom, it is best to align the bed north/south in keeping with the body's own magnetic field and it should not be directly opposite the door or it will drain your energy. Bedside lamps should also be placed next to the bed and not over it so they do not interfere with the electrical field. If it isn't possible to align the bed north/south, sleep with your head facing east. A bed should stand off the ground so there is a healthy flow of air and ch'i below it. Do not sleep regularly on a bed set with storage drawers below as this will affect the quality of your sleep. If you require the storage area below the bed, place it in a spare room for overnight guests.

Bathrooms should be kept to one side of the house rather than in a central position. This is a sensible idea as bad odors and dampness need to escape outside. For the same reason, kitchens need to have access to an outside wall and window. A square or rectangular kitchen works best, especially if it is on the south or east side of the house. A kitchen facing a bathroom or toilet will encourage bad health. South relates to the fire element and east is the position of family and health.

Doors

The doorway is the protector of the house, keeping out the wind and rain and strangers. Doors and windows are the eyes and ears of your home which form both the dividing line and connection with the outside world. When approaching a house, the size and shapes of the doors and windows will have a strong effect on you. They should give out a welcoming message to you and your visitors, while protecting you against harmful energies and unwanted spirits.

The transition between the home and the outside should not be abrupt. We need an in-between space where we can orient ourselves and prepare for the change in energy. A path, steps, plants, fences and gates allow us time to adjust. In many cultures, you remove your shoes before entering the house. This is both a spiritual and practical ritual. By taking off shoes you ensure that the negative vibrations clinging to them remain in a porch or outer area, and you also prevent muddy shoes leaving unsightly footprints on the floor.

In the East, it is traditional for the front door to face the rising sun and it is decorated with good luck charms or colors which ward off evil. If you are replacing a front door, or creating a new one, it is worth considering the importance of the threshold.

A good front door should be both attractive and functional. Doors should always fit snugly and be well maintained. Valuable ch'i energy can be lost through ill-fitting doors,

TO ATTRACT WEALTH, BOOST THE WATER ELEMENTS BY INTRODUCING AN AQUARIUM INTO YOUR HOME. AN UNEVEN NUMBER OF GOLDFISH IS AN EFFECTIVE WAY OF COMBATING MALIGN INFLUENCES.

and this dispersed energy can be harmful to the occupants of the house. If you are going to replace any doors in your home try to match them with the old ones as long as these are attractive and in keeping with the building style. Matching your doors will enhance the atmosphere and add a unifying force to your home.

Windows

The window is the source of a home's fresh air and light and a space which allows us to connect to the outside world. It is through the windows that the inhabitants of the house view the changes of the seasons and the passage of time.

To amplify ch'i energy into the home through the windows, you can hang crystals and prisms in positions that catch the sun and reflect beautiful rainbows of light into a room. Hanging crystal pendants in this way are extremely beneficial in a dark room which needs enhancing with color and light. You can also find lovely stained or painted glass panels to hang in windows, and the filtered light pouring through these will have a similar energizing effect. To ward off unwanted energies from the outside, small mirrors or beads with mirrored surfaces can deflect bad vibrations.

Feng shui cures

If you discover that the ch'i is blocked in your present home it is not necessary to move to another house where there is good feng shui. There are many ways you can deflect negative energy and promote a good flow of ch'i.

Here are nine of the basic feng shui cures which you can use to restore harmonious vibrations.

Plants

There are many ways that plants can help you enhance the feng shui in your home. Plants absorb and store light vibrations from the sun, transforming and transmitting ch'i into the air around them. Where there is free-flowing ch'i, plants will flourish and so will the inhabitants of the building. So plants are good indicators of whether your home has good or bad feng shui.

Plants with large rounded green leaves will help alleviate suffering from financial problems. The growth of the plant will reflect the upward turn of your fortunes. The larger the plant, the larger the fortune. Plants with pointed leaves act as knives which cut your fortunes. If, however, you have a low ceiling you may encourage the upward movement of ch'i by getting some plants with vertical lines and which point upwards.

Living objects

Ch'i is related to the earth although it is not of the earth itself. It is related to the energy and life-force which courses through the earth. So the rocks and minerals are alive with this earth energy. Humankind can link to these other forms of life by slowing down our brainwaves through contemplation and

GARDEN PATHS SHOULD MEANDER BECAUSE ENERGY THAT TRAVELS IN A STRAIGHT LINE IS TOO DISORIENTATING. A GENTLY CURVING PATH ALLOWS YOU TIME TO ADJUST TO THE CHANGE IN ENERGY BETWEEN THE OUTSIDE AND INSIDE OF THE HOUSE.

ENHANCING THE WELCOME AND PROTECTION AFFORDED BY YOUR FRONT DOOR

☞ Place a welcome mat outside the front door.

☞ Make a path leading up to the door, planted on either side with aromatic shrubs, trees or flowers.

☞ Find a door knocker in the shape of your favorite animal or symbol (see page 115).

☞ Get a brass bell or bell pull so that the sound of the door bell is pleasing and musical.

☞ Stained-glass panels with a design incorporating the sun's rays or other symbol can be a welcoming sight when you come home. Include your protective angel, animal or prayer in some way in the door or frame.

☞ Paint the door in a welcoming color of your choice.

SOME CAUSES OF BAD FENG SHUI

☞ Bent or weak door frame: the family's fortunes will suffer.

☞ Tree or post in front of front door: financial loss will occur because of broken ch'i.

☞ Main door facing the corner of another house or dead-end street: they are like daggers and cause ill health and financial loss.

☞ Main door facing a church or cemetery: these provide refuge for homeless spirits.

☞ A gap in two buildings facing the house: your savings will slowly fritter away.

☞ View of the sitting room from the front door: in a large room, obscure part of the view with a piece of furniture; a small room is okay if you hang a mirror to create space, but make sure the bottom of a staircase is not reflected.

☞ Kitchen facing a bathroom or toilet: encourages bad health.

☞ Stove next to a window: wind can extinguish gas and the sun may spoil the food.

meditation. This allows us to become sensitive to the vibrations of these living objects.

Our brains function using beta waves most of the time. These have a very fast wavelength which is suited to our brain capacity and the need to be flexible and adaptable. When you sleep, the mind is relaxed and the brain wave pattern changes to the slower alpha wave pattern. Because plants are stationary, they emit theta waves which are much slower still, and slowest of all are living objects from the mineral kingdom. Their life force is typified by delta waves. These delta waves set up a slow undercurrent of energy which can pervade your home.

Stones and rocks placed carefully in your home have a stabilizing effect on the ch'i in the room. If you tune in to these vibrations you will benefit from the feeling of security which they can give you. If you have trouble holding down a job or stabilizing a relationship, heavy objects can be of assistance. A statue made of wood or stone will have the effect of bringing you down to earth. Once you draw back into the hearth and the home, which is symbolic of the center of yourself, you can best discover your real identity and true path in life.

Water

In the Chinese elemental system, water symbolizes money. By introducing water into your home its energy will attract life-giving and wealth-making ch'i.

Ground water will have the most powerful effect on the ch'i within your home.

Water in the form of natural water courses and rivers are of great importance, since they are one of the natural features of the landscape which can influence our well-being. The shapes of the 'water dragon', as it is called, can be either beneficial or have adverse effects on us.

For instance, the point where two rivers meet has a beneficial effect as this concentrates the influences. Branches of a river, however, indicate the points where the energy is dissipated. A sharp bend in the river is unlucky, while a gentle meandering river has a positive influence.

If you do not live near a river, a pond or pool can be influential. Adding a water feature like a fountain to your garden in the right place can also attract positive forces. A pond in your front garden will have this positive influence as long as it is not too large.

You can introduce the water element indoors too. An aquarium containing an uneven number of goldfish is an effective way of combating malign influences and converting negative spirits to positive ones. If this is not possible, a bowl of water in which you float flowers helps balance your emotions. You could even add a vase of flowers, but first add a crystal to the water (see page 110). This not only makes cut flowers last longer but sends out healing vibrations into the room.

Mirrors

Mirrors strategically placed can deflect bad feng shui and amplify good vibrations into a building or room. Small and dark rooms benefit by placing mirrors opposite any opening or direction of natural light and to reflect good views of water or gardens. A mirror attached to the back of a door at the end of a corridor or passageway stops energy draining through the building. If the main piece of furniture in a room faces away from the door, a mirror placed in a position where it reflects the entrance to the room can provide protection for the occupants. This works in the same way as a rear view mirror in a car.

If you discover a dead energy spot in a corner of your home, either by dowsing or another means, reflect positive energy into that corner by directing a mirror towards that spot. Mirror tiles on a ceiling will deflect energy downwards, so make sure you are aware what type of energy is in the room, or you will be doubling its strength.

Wind chimes and bells

Sound and air are the two elements we often ignore when designing or arranging our homes. This is probably because they are not tangible things in the same way as color and furnishings. Sound vibrations are very powerful. We all know that the human voice can shatter glass when pitched at a certain note. This is because sound vibrations set up a resonance that is picked up by the atoms and molecules with which they come into contact. If you have two guitars in the same room and you strike a string on one of them, the vibratory pattern of the note will cause the second guitar string to vibrate in the same way, making the same sound. Consequently, this ability of sound to influence matter means that it can also move and change other energy patterns.

Wind chimes and bells can be used to summon up ch'i into the home. If the vibrations in a room are very dense and heavy, music or other sounds can literally clear the air. Wind chimes can move energy into areas which are stagnant, such as rooms that have been closed up for a long time or have a strong presence of someone who has used them in the past.

Both bells and wind chimes when placed at an entrance or doorway act as warning alarms against intruders. They can also be used to keep out bad vibrations. Mirrors alone are not always powerful enough to deflect bad fortune from your home, and when this is the case, a wind chime used together with a mirror can be hung outside your front door. You can do this in instances where you live opposite a graveyard or have a large building or tree in front of your home. Wind chimes can be made of many different materials. Wood or bamboo create a soft woody sound, while shells or ceramics give a stronger, higher sound.

Lights and crystal balls

Light is auspicious as it is the life-giver, so lighting in the home and garden is a powerful feng shui cure. The light emitted from artificial lamps is in itself energy and it can enhance interior ch'i. Indoor light represents the sun and the brighter the lamp, the more powerful is its clearing and enhancing effect within the room.

Another way of bringing light into the home is by hanging crystal pendants in a window. These refract natural light into prismatic colors which disperse positive ch'i around the room. The energy of these powerful vibrations has the effect of transforming threatening vibrations, helping to lift the energy in the entire home. The quality of the life led by the occupants will subsequently be generally improved.

SOME CAUSES OF BAD FENG SHUI (CONT)

☞ Stove next to a sink or refrigerator: elements of fire and water will clash.

☞ Sofa or bed lies directly under a beam: headaches, mental disorders and loss of creative energy will occur.

☞ Bed directly opposite the door: drains your energy.

☞ Bed opposite a mirror: causes bad temper and emotional problems.

☞ Lights over the bed: damage eyesight and cause liver disease.

☞ Storage under the bed: brings ill health.

☞ Central bathroom: bad odors from yin spirits (water) will permeate through the house.

Colors

In feng shui, certain colors are more auspicious than others and these relate to the five elements. Objects or decor colored in these colors can also be located at different points in a room, corresponding with the directions of the compass (see box, right).

Flutes and ribbons

The sound of a flute is one which is light and clear. It heralds good news and brings peace and safety. In the home, it is associated with security and stability and is often hung for protection and to discourage intruders. A flute can symbolically lift the ch'i of a house and, when shaken, drive away evil spirits.

Red ribbons can also be tied around various objects to provide protection. The oppressive influence of a beam can be moderated by attaching two flutes tied with red ribbons so that the flutes lean towards each other. This has the effect of drawing the ch'i upward. Red ribbons can also be tied to door knobs or hung over doorways or beams. These will assist in protecting whatever aspect of your home they are attached to.

Mobiles

Cities emit low-frequency sounds that permeate our systems in a damaging way. Inharmonious sound vibrations can interfere with our own body rhythms and energy system. The movement of mobiles deflects negative forces, preventing them from building up in long corridors or stagnant corners.

A STATUE MADE OF MARBLE OR STONE CAN HAVE A STABILIZING INFLUENCE ON THE HOME.

WHAT'S IN A COLOR

Black
North; relates to money, but also to loss of light.

White
West; is the color of mourning.

Blue
Northeast; relates to the water element but also the sky.

Yellow
Center; represents longevity and health.

Green
East; is the color of spring and new growth, tranquility.

Red
South; is the fire element that links to the heart and to summer.

The Natural Home

Every time we turn on a tap or light switch we interact with the environment. This is not something 'out there' which is separate from us. We are affecting and reacting to the natural and man-made systems around us; we are an integral part of the world and its ecology. This vision of our planet as a cooperation and balance between all things forms the basis of the 'Gaia' movement which emerged in the 1980s. Gaia was inspired by a book by James Lovelock, called *New Look at Life on Earth*, where he describes the earth and its life systems as a living organism.

The damage we are causing our natural environment is affecting our health and psychological well-being. Self-help groups abound and many people are genuinely trying to lead a healthier and more stress-free life. Unfortunately, although so much time, money and energy is spent finding a more holistic lifestyle, very few of us extend this more caring approach to our home environment. Like us, our home needs to be integrated into the natural processes around it and be part of the chain and flow of materials and energy.

There is an increasing awareness of the importance in the quality of our surroundings. The colors and materials used in modern buildings affect our well-being, as do the shapes, size and proportions of our homes and cities. For the most part, architects and planners have forgotten that our environment should not only be aesthetically attractive, but that scale has an important effect on us physically and psychologically.

The house is a perfect expression of the self, and the way we use space is a key to understanding our inner selves. The history of human consciousness can be interpreted through our buildings, from the circular shelters of primitive people to contemporary, urban, rectangular structures. The square represents man, but is also a symbol of the Earth to which he belongs. The circle represents man's origins. To build a house is to create an area of peace, calm and security which is a replica of our mother's womb. It is a place where we can leave the world, safe from any external dangers.

If we are to truly understand and develop our self-knowledge and spirituality, we have to put our beliefs into practice. To start with, we can use harmless substances instead of those that damage the natural world through high energy costs and toxic emissions in their manufacture. This means changing our habits to create a healing home, and using environmentally friendly materials is one way of doing this. Natural materials come in an array of beautiful colors, textures and smells. They are easy to create and apply and have no harmful by-products. They are also micro-porous, anti-static and anti-allergic and do not require testing on animals. Disposing of them is no problem either as they are biodegradable.

Many people avoid natural materials because they think they look too rustic or old-fashioned. In fact, scientists are developing many modern materials which are environmentally friendly, such as a plastic that is developed from oil-seed rape instead of mineral oil. Whereas traditional oil is expensive, hard to exploit, can involve spillage and is a finite resource, oil-seed rape is renewable and economic to produce. At the time of writing this book, however, no environmental studies on large-scale planting of oil-seed rape have been done. It is up to us to inquire about such new products at local suppliers so we can encourage products of this kind.

Natural materials also emit subtle vibrations which are in harmony with our own and link us to other kingdoms which share this planet. The soothing and harmonious vibrations these materials emit can help us redress the balance and the harmony which our lives have lost.

A SIMPLE, RUSTIC KITCHEN CAN BE MADE FROM RECYCLED BOARDS WHICH HARMONIZE WITH THE NATURAL MATERIALS IN THE ADJOINING ROOM.

Natural materials

COLORING PAINT

Try coloring paint yourself using natural pigments. This is great fun and works out much cheaper than buying commercially produced products. Use porous paint for the base in an off-white color and buy some powdered or tubes of natural pigments. A basic palette, which should be sufficient to make most colors, consists of Venetian red, alizarin crimson, vermilion, Prussian blue, ultramarine, cobalt, cerulean blue, chrome yellow, cadmium yellow, yellow ochre, viridian, emerald green, Van Dyke brown, raw sienna, burnt sienna, burnt umber and lamp black. It is very easy to add a single or mixture of colors to your base paint, a little at a time, until you reach the desired tone.

So what do we mean by basic, natural materials? Most are cheap, readily available and can be used in a wide variety of ways to enhance our homes. First there are natural paints and varnishes and then there are products derived from nature in the raw. These are derived from minerals (stone, slate and limestone, and marble), earth (bricks, tiles and ceramics) and plants (timber, cane and grass, and natural fibers).

Paints and varnishes

With most of us spending 80 per cent of our time indoors, a healthy room climate, free of poisonous emissions or long-term untested synthetics, is of paramount importance to support a strong immune system.

Microporous finishes, prepared from natural raw materials and colored with natural pigments, provide a healthy and friendly atmosphere to any work or living space. Microporous finishes allow mineral and wooden surfaces to breath and maintain their long-term structure. Moisture exchange helps to provide the right atmosphere for our own and our house's long-term well-being. Paint made from natural resin and organic origins contains no solvents or odor, so is particularly good for allergy sufferers and the very young or weak. You can add aromatic oils to natural paints which will linger in the room, creating a soft aroma.

Contrary to popular belief, you can obtain organic oil-based gloss paints. These can be used on stone, metal or wood, both inside and outside the home. An organic masonry paint is also available for exterior stone and plasterwork.

Traditional varnishes are made from natural resins, linseed oil and thinners. Lazur is a natural product which is translucent and can be used for wood protection. This varnish is microporous, allowing the wood to breathe while still being impervious to water.

If you have to use synthetic oil-based paints and varnishes, use them sparingly and only in dry warm weather. Make sure you open the doors and windows to allow the fumes to escape. Remember to remove as much furniture and furnishings as possible as these absorb the toxic chemicals. There are some synthetic microporous paints available which allow the underlying plaster, stone or wood to breathe.

Although pure turpentine is obtained from many species of conifer tree, use turpentine substitute or white spirit instead. Pure turpentine emits strong fumes which can cause your eyes to water and other types of allergic reactions, while the substitute and white spirit is distilled from a resinous oil derived from balsa wood or citrus peels.

Shellac is a pure resin varnish which is useful as a sealant. Paint on a coat of shellac over chemically treated building materials such as composite or plasterboard and it will seal the fumes. Shellac provides a very good base on which to use various decorative paint effects on walls. Its sealing qualities stop the surface from absorbing the glaze or color wash, allowing you time to manipulate the surface to form your pattern.

White paint is the most widely used paint in the world and was originally made from white lead which is poisonous. Now it has been superseded by the use of zinc and titanium white pigment. Titanium ore is more stable and unaffected by heat, light and air and is now the largest selling white pigment used in paints and dyes. You can buy a very soft white paint which contains no titanium dioxide but you still need to check that paints and varnishes are lead free. This paint is ideal for using as a base to which you can add various natural tints.

Brilliant white used be the most popular paint until the 'Hint of a Tint' range of subtly shaded white paints came on the market. This suggested a growing trend away from the sterile, modern environment where emphasis is placed on hygiene. When you think of it, a white environment can be as frightening as a black one. This is evident in the move away from all-white hospital rooms and those found in mental institutions, schools and other public places. People have now discovered that living in a white environment is clinical and gives little emotional support. Thankfully there is a trend to introduce a palette of livelier color into our lives. Instead, white paint is probably best used as a neutral background to colorful furnishings and to provide contrast to brighter colors, especially when used on woodwork and ceilings.

Stone, slate and limestone

Stone and slate are very beautiful natural materials which are plentiful and locally obtainable. Limestone and slate tiles can be used for floors in kitchens, halls, conservatories and swimming pool areas and come in a wide variety of colors such as dark gray, green, red, purple and multicolored. Bear in mind that both slate and stone are cold to the touch, and if used in living areas in colder climates it is best to use scatter rugs of thick wool or cotton.

Slate and stone are extremely hard-wearing and require little maintenance so can be used very successfully as a roofing material as well as being incorporated into a hearth or fireplace.

Marble

The natural beauty of marble is very appealing to most of us but we may not be aware that it is expensive to produce. Traveling recently by train in Tuscany, I was horrified to see the damage caused by the marble quarries; whole hillsides had been gouged away. Although many of the wonders of antiquity have utilized marble, we are fast using up this exquisite natural resource.

If you wish to use marble in your home, use it sparingly. Marble is a surprisingly soft material, and can easily be damaged and stained. It is also very porous, so does not do well in a constantly wet area.

BRINGING THE MINERAL KINGDOM INTO YOUR HOME

❧ Collect river or beach pebbles and place them around your plants.

❧ Fill an ornamental bottle with colored sand or shells.

❧ Display a decorative bowl filled with semi-precious stones.

❧ Find an interesting large stone and use it as a doorstop.

❧ Buy a natural quartz or amethyst cluster for your living room.

❧ Use a marble tile as a pastry board as it is easier to roll out dough that is kept nice and cold.

NATURAL WAYS TO RESTORE
WOOD AND KEEP IT GLOWING

✍ On stripped pine floors and other soft woods, prime the wood using two coats of primer, especially in heavy traffic areas like halls, kitchens and bathrooms. Then apply three coats of varnish (the first coat should be diluted with 20% turpentine). Alternatively, limewash the natural wood with liming paste and then seal.

✍ Neutralize stripped pine doors and windows with vinegar and water, if necessary after stripping. Brush on 'Herb and Resin' oil generously, wipe off any residue with lint-free cloth. This will nourish and enliven any 'dead' or dry-looking wood. Leave to dry, or repeat several coats for a more shiny, oiled finish. Alternatively, wax the wood thinly with furniture wax and polish.

✍ Treat oak or hardwood floors with a primer, followed by waxing with a natural floor wax. Re-wax approximately once a year.

Bricks, tiles and ceramics

In industrialized nations, our earth connection has been slowly eroded. Generations of parents have told their children not to get their hands dirty and discouraged their sons and daughters from playing with soil or mud. In their effort to keep clothes clean, children are growing up deprived of a vital sensory experience and earth connection. Instead of walking bare foot on the ground, we put on shoes. Rather than sit on the floor, we have designed furniture that places us in the air and many of our homes are in tower blocks well away from the ground. No wonder we often feel insecure and lose our sense of belonging in the world.

For thousands of years, humanity has made shelters from the natural materials he found in his surroundings. Earth has been the most basic element, and this connection with the earth has made clay a perfect medium for building a home. Earth buildings absorb the heat of the sun during the day, while radiating it during the night. This means that earth has excellent insulating qualities. It is also an abundant material and costs little to obtain.

Earthenware building materials have an individual and particular texture and grain. Clay bricks and tiles are warm to touch and are made from a breathing material. Earth tiles have the natural coloring of the earth from the area in which the clay is found.

Glazed roof and floor tiles have been used in buildings from China to South America for many centuries and tile fire surrounds have been popular in Europe for many centuries. The beautiful colors and patterned tiles can help create a home full of warmth and inter-esting features. There are many beautiful earthenware pots and ceramic articles we can buy from local potters and craft shops. So if your home is short of the earth connection, fill it with decorative items made from clay.

Timber

Wood is a sacred commodity and one that is running short. We are losing thousands of acres of natural forests and woodlands every day. Trees not only create oxygen but bring our planet great joy and beauty. They protect and nourish our planet at all levels and it is vital for our own well-being and that of future generations that we honor and protect this wonder of nature. Timber is a living, breathing material. Wood is also scented, warm and soothing on our emotions.

One of the best ways to connect with wood in the home is to walk bare foot on wooden floorboards. Feel the strength entering your being through your feet and rising up your legs into your spine. Care lovingly for wood as it will bring healing and peaceful vibrations to your home. Wood is created by the earth element and supports the element of fire. So it has a special place in the cycle of universal order and energy flow.

Wood is a gentle but strong natural material. The sound it makes when struck also has a soothing and calming quality. Use natural wood in the kitchen as worktops or as a chopping board. As you hold a wooden spoon or bowl in your hands feel how humble the living tree was in providing such a great service to you.

Certain woods have beautiful aromas, which can permeate a drawer or cupboard.

Cedar wood acts as a moth repellent, while sandalwood exudes a rich Oriental perfume.

When using wood in the home, try to select used timbers. Old wood is seasoned and hardened and much more beautiful in terms of color than new wood. Old furniture is better made than new factory-produced items and is cheap by comparison. Even antiques cost less than modern reproductions, as wood and labor costs have risen dramatically over the last few decades.

If you wish to buy new wood for flooring, cladding or furniture, check that it is well seasoned and is not a protected hardwood variety. Ask your supplier to find out the origin of the timber so you can be sure it is not tropical hardwood. New wood should preferably be locally produced, and hardwoods should be indigenous. During the storms in England a few years ago, many trees were blown over and others had to be cut for reasons of safety. As a result, cabinet makers and joiners suddenly had a supply of lovely English hardwoods at their disposal. Some of this wood has been used to create sculptures and pieces of furniture which are now becoming available on the market but can be rather expensive.

If you are fortunate enough to have trees in your garden, you can connect to their positive vibrations. It is best to do this in the early morning or at sunset when negative ions in the air are at their greatest levels. Stand with your back against a tree with a straight trunk so you connect to its strength and power. You may prefer to place your hands on the trunk while looking up into the branches and leaves. The tree will send out its particular healing vibrations to you.

Just as trees and flowers can help us care for ourselves, we need to care for them in return if we are to benefit from their healing vibrations. Many building materials as well as furniture and furnishings in our homes are made from trees or timber products and these need to be nourished and cared for if they are to serve us well. If we do this, wood can improve with age. It can shine and mellow and give out loving energy for years.

Cane and grass

Bamboo and cane can be used extensively in the natural home and items made from these materials are both attractive and inexpensive. Furniture made from cane comes in many designs and colors, creating a warm but simple interior style. Wicker and rattan furniture from the Far East can introduce a touch of the exotic and look especially good in garden rooms and patios. Screens, blinds and lamp shades made of paper or slatted cane softly filter sunlight, making them suitable for rooms where you want an even, non-reflecting light.

Unfortunately, wicker furniture is at risk if you have a cat or puppy as claw marks and chewing can be a problem, but bent cane is much stronger and more durable to family wear and tear. Bamboo fibers can also be woven into matting to make attractive floorcoverings and could be used for yoga or when practicing relaxation techniques.

The fibers of the coconut palm and other plants are often used to make rope and cloth, and are now gaining in popularity for floorcoverings. Coir has tough, coarse fibers and is strong and hardwearing, although on the

NATURAL WAYS TO RESTORE WOOD AND KEEP IT GLOWING (CONT)

✍ On wooden furniture, use a herb and resin oil wood nourisher to treat dry or old wood like window frames, doors and beams. Commercially produced oil is available from a number of suppliers and provides a water repellent and anti-fungal finish. Use this before waxing.

✍ Wax can be made from beeswax and linseed oil to which you can add a few drops of your favorite essential oil, which will give a lustrous and aromatic finish. You can also protect your wooden furniture from becoming dry and prevent beetle infestations by treating with a mixture of borax, soda, potash, linseed oil and beeswax.

A BEDROOM CAN OFFER A PLACE
OF REST AND TRANQUILITY
AWAY FROM THE FAMILY.

floor it can be quite hard and scratchy. Sisal is extracted from long leaf fibers and makes a softer alternative. Jute is primarily used to make hessian (burlap) which makes a good natural backing for carpeting, wall coverings and linoleum. Seagrass matting is attractive and durable but requires periodic watering to prevent it from cracking and drying out!

All types of natural matting have an uneven texture, which can be very therapeutic to walk on bare foot. Our feet have for generations been covered in socks, stockings and shoes. Is it any wonder we have lost our earth connections? Walking on a rough natural material gently massages the foot, developing our sensitivity to touch through this part of our body. It is through the ground that we receive many electromagnetic vibrations, sound and heat. Developing your foot sensitivity will help you connect to these earth energies, helping you release pent-up negative energy and receive strengthening and nourishing vibrations.

Natural fibers

Natural fibers have vibrations in keeping with our own. When used as clothing, they allow light and air to pass freely through them, so our skin can breathe and vital light energy enters the body. Using natural fabrics in home furnishings has similar effects. Light, air and aroma can pass freely through them and the fabrics themselves will not contribute to indoor pollution.

Linen, cotton, wool and silk form the basis of natural fibers which can be used in our homes. Cotton is the most important vegetable fiber which is taken from the bolls of the cotton plant, and when tightly spun has greater strength than wool. Linen is the oldest known fabric and those unearthed in early Egyptian tombs were woven of linen. It is a vegetable fiber made from flax and its long fibers makes a smooth and lustrous yarn. One of the oldest and most beautiful fibers is silk. The strands of silk unraveled from the silk moth cocoon are finer than a human hair. Wool has been produced for centuries from the fleece of sheep and other animals and while it is resilient and strong it is also incredibly soft.

Unfortunately, many natural fibers are produced using chemicals and pesticides and often synthetic dyes are used to color cloth. When buying a natural cloth, try to find a source which states the manufacturing process. Choose colors which are found in nature and you will be more likely to find cloth dyed with natural dyes.

Natural living rooms

The hearth has always been the focal point of the home. It is the heart of the home where people gather and enjoy each other's company and warmth. Even today a brightly burning fire is an immediate attraction and homes with fireplaces have an immediate feeling of focus and exude warm vibrations. The chimney provides a channel up to the heavens and into the air, and it is via the chimney that good and bad spirits can have access to your home. As long as we burn environmentally friendly fuel, having a fireplace still remains a powerful focal point of the home.

If you are building a fireplace, try to fit it with a high-performance combustion stove.

WALKING BAREFOOT ON A
WOODEN FLOOR RENEWS OUR
EARTH CONNECTION AND
SENSITIVITY TO THE NATURAL
WORLD.

HELPING TO CREATE HARMONY
WITHIN THE HOME

✎ Bring in plants for peace and tranquillity.

✎ Hang peaceful and loving pictures.

✎ Fabric or woven hanging or rugs give warmth, grounding and security.

✎ Clocks provide harmony and rhythm.

✎ A piano or musical instrument gives social or personal empathy and compassion.

✎ Natural objects are healing and provide feeling of connection.

✎ Wind chimes give sound and rhythm, variety and balance.

✎ A water feature is emotionally soothing and healing.

✎ Light fittings provide sparkling light and inspiration or create a more intimate atmosphere.

These stoves increase the heat output while minimizing the pollutants emitted. You can get a variety of different stoves which burn either smokeless fuel or wood. In a modern home, you may consider installing a gas open fire. These fires do not give out much heat, and really only serve the function of enjoying natural flames. So make sure that you are not relying on an open gas fire for your entire source of winter heating. You may still wish to add a more traditional mantle, which will harmonize with the style of the building.

Wooden floors create a peaceful environment and are warm to the touch. If you need to cover wooden floors to help with sound proofing, choose a natural floorcovering. Wool carpet is best although you may prefer a covering made of cork, linoleum, sisal, coir or seagrass. Do not stick vinyl floor tiles onto a wooden floor as this prevents the floor from breathing and encourages dampness. The fumes and vibrations given off by plastic- and rubber-based materials can be toxic and affect the health of the occupants.

Natural kitchens and dining rooms

People always tend to gather in an area where there is warmth and nourishment. They may sit in front of a roaring fire or gravitate to the dining or kitchen table. Every home needs an area like this where family and friends can gather, a place that is both comfortable and mellow. Unfortunately, our modern desire to streamline the preparation of meals and our concern with hygiene has led us to create kitchens and dining rooms that can be frighteningly cold and clinical.

The modern kitchen is often wasteful of water and energy (for ways around this see page 42) and does not recycle valuable waste materials. A well-designed kitchen may be functional, but it can also be an attractive and appealing space. Think of your kitchen holistically, paying attention to the whole rather than individual parts. Try making your kitchen into a workplace, family headquarters and social center.

You spend many hours on your feet in the kitchen, so flooring can make a difference as to whether you come away worn out and tired, or relaxed and ready to enjoy the remainder of the day.

Wood is the best choice for a natural kitchen floor. Wood is warm and earthy and soft on the feet. It protects you from winter chills and is a delight to the eye. You will need to sand and seal the wood so that it is easy to clean. Make sure you use a natural wood sealer or varnish. If you are refurbishing, try to locate some used timbers. They often come in different lengths and widths and are therefore much cheaper than commercially produced modern timber. Old timber has personality and works very well for a country-style kitchen in an older house.

If you cannot use wood, you can buy very attractive linoleum in sheets or tiles. Linoleum is a natural product, so choose this instead of vinyl tiles as these are plastic-based and chemicals are used in its production. Carpet is less suitable in a kitchen although you may wish to use a natural carpet in a dining area. Remember food is difficult to clean off carpets and natural floorcoverings like sisal and coir. Try to choose a smooth natural surface for your kitchen floor.

Quarry, slate and terracotta tiles all make good floor tiles which can harmonize with an older style house. Although they are made from natural materials, these tiles can be cold and hard on the feet. You can always put colorful rugs and mats on floor tiles in the kitchen as these are easy to shake out and wash. They can add a warm, friendly feeling to your kitchen.

Natural bedrooms

Make sure your bedroom is not overcrowded with furniture and has plenty of cupboard space as this will allow air and ch'i to flow freely around the room.

The bed is the most important piece of furniture in the bedroom, so take time and care when you are selecting one. Make sure it affords your back just the right amount of support and that any internal springs do not create any magnetic disturbance (see geopathic stress on page 48). A bad bed can put strain on your spine and also affect the quality of your sleep and consequently your energy levels throughout the following day. It is also most important to use natural materials on your bedcovers and curtaining, as well as on the floor and walls of your bedroom.

Your bedroom can often be a place where you can find rest and tranquillity away from the family. Try to create a definite relaxation area here, perhaps in a corner of the room or near a window. Place a comfortable chair and a small table where you could enjoy a breakfast or cup of tea in this space, enjoying the peaceful view stretching away in front of you. You can screen this area from the rest of the room with a decorative screen of plants.

Natural bathrooms

Although en suite bathrooms have gained popularity, these usually have hard divisions separating them from the bedroom. While it is convenient to have a shower and sink next to the bedroom, too often the bath is squeezed into a small, airless space. This means that bathing for the most part takes place in cramped conditions. I feel that a toilet should never be en suite as it will lack privacy and bad odors invariably permeate into the bedroom. But the bath itself does not need to be entirely separate from the bedroom. Creating a bathroom adjoining a bedroom could mean changing the level of the floor or using a low screen of plants as a soft divider. Ideally, the bath should be housed in a good-sized room with plenty of natural light and, if possible, a view!

If you are replacing the original bath and sink, a modern metal bath is the best option. Choose tiles made of clay or decorated in warm soothing colors as these create a feeling of warmth and are in natural harmony with our body vibrations. An all white or black bathroom can be cold and draining. These color energies make you feel uncomfortable and will not encourage you to linger in the bathroom. Use natural materials like wood and plants to create a restful and relaxing space. Lights should be soft, and light bulbs have a yellow or peachy tint. Avoid fluorescent fittings above a mirror as this light makes the skin look gray and unhealthy. The flickering of strip lights sets up disturbing vibrations which can make us ill. Your aim should be to create a truly relaxing bathroom – see the Hydrotherapy chapter on pages 92-9.

WASTE

Here are some ways to cut down on waste and make your kitchen a healthier and friendlier place:

☙ Try to buy fresh food as often as you can. This reduces the need for storage.

☙ Use natural washing-up liquid and scouring powders.

☙ Sort rubbish into organic matter and waste that can be recycled such as bottles, paper and tins.

☙ Wash up by hand.

☙ Avoid plastic wrap which can give off vapors, especially when food is hot. Instead, use glass, ceramic and stainless steel containers to store food.

☙ Keep food in a cool, dry larder or cellar and perishables in the refrigerator.

☙ Get a water filter: either a jug or a water filter fitted to your tap.

☙ Do not buy over-packaged food; and take your own bag, egg box or bottle, for example.

The Color Sanctuary

Every person feels uplifted when they are put in a light and bright environment, and color is the first and most important means of creating a relaxed and harmonious atmosphere around us.

Color vibrations come to earth as part of the electromagnetic spectrum contained in pure white sunlight. Each color vibration has a different wavelength and strong effect on us. The colored rays affect not only our physical body but also our emotions, moods and mental frame of mind. Certain colors can be spiritually uplifting and inspiring, helping us connect with the cosmic forces around us.

Every cell in our body is light sensitive and also gives off its own light vibrations. Color not only enters our eyes, but also enters our body through our skin. Clothing acts as a light filter and the different color clothes you wear will allow different wavelengths of color to permeate through them. We experience the colors in our surroundings visually and their effect is absorbed through our aura. The aura is made up of light and sound vibrations emitted by all our cells, glands and organs, so our general state of our health is revealed by the array and proportions of colors in the aura.

The colors surrounding us in our home should be in harmony with our own auric color vibrations. Then we can relax. People with strong personalities will like bright, strong colors, whereas softer personalities will prefer light, pastel shades. Your color preferences will mirror the colors in your aura.

ORANGE WALLS IN A DINING ROOM ENCOURAGE CREATIVITY, STIMULATE THE APPETITE AND PROMOTE SOCIAL INTERACTION.

Your Identity Color

COMPLEMENTARY COLORS

A complementary color
is the color which is the natural
opposing but balancing color
energy. When two
complementary colors are
mixed together as light, they
form white light.
To find a complementary color,
look at a color wheel and you
will see that red is
complementary to blue, yellow
is complementary to violet, blue
is complementary to orange,
and magenta is complementary
to green.

If you need to find an exact
complementary shade, color a
square of paper in the main
decorating color. Now place this
square next to a piece of clean
white paper. Stare at the colored
paper for thirty seconds or so
and then look quickly at the
white paper. On it you will see
an after-image. This will be the
exact complementary color. If
you have a color chart or cards
handy, try to find one that most
closely resembles this color and
tone.

The colors in our aura change over a period of time, and the shapes and arrangements of the colors are affected by our immediate moods and emotions. We do, however, have certain colors which we feel comfortable with all our lives. These colors are those which are in harmony with our inner vibrations and which I call 'soul colors'.

To find out your soul colors, ask yourself the following question: 'If I were a color, what color would I be?' If you think that the color light blue best represents you, then that is your soul color. The second way you can find what your auric colors are, is to write down the two colors you wear most often. These usually remain constant over a long period of time and you can make use of them in the color scheme of your home.

Most of us have a preference for either cool colors such as blues and greens, or for warm colors such as peach and yellow. The tone of the color will also attract or repel us. Decide whether you feel happier surrounded by pastels, light but bright colors, or rich, darker tones. You should now have at least three colors to work with, and have identified a group of colors or tones you prefer.

There might also be a color which has recently become appealing to you. You may have bought an item for the house or article of clothing which is different from your usual color choice. It is likely you need this color energy at this time, and you can introduce elements of this color into your home for inspiration. As this new color preference is likely to be a passing attraction, it is best to introduce it in some impermanent way. You could buy some flowers of this color, or a gemstone, ornament or cushion. Having the object reflecting this color close to you during the day will have a positive effect on your general well-being. You will then ingest the color energy you need through your eyes, skin or from the air. If you choose flowers of a certain color you will absorb the subtle color vibrations through their scent.

Changing your life

Often the colors we choose to have around us are, in fact, reflecting our own bad moods and disharmony. These colors can be detrimental to our physical and mental health. This is especially true if we are feeling depressed, unhappy or lonely. People who feel down often surround themselves with dark colors. What they need, however, are lighter and brighter colors to lift them out of their depression.

Attraction to new colors can signify a change in your outlook and personal growth. These are the colors you are drawn to as your auric colors change. If you have a strong attraction to a color which you have not felt before you can try painting a wall or room in this color. It may be that it is your true identity color or that you are growing and the new you will thrive on this color. By changing the colors around you, you will change your life for the better.

THE POSITIVE AND NEGATIVE QUALITIES OF COLOR

COLOR	PERSONALITY	POSITIVE QUALITIES	NEGATIVE QUALITIES
Red	outgoing, active, physical	motivating, warming	irritable, anger
Orange	sociable, creative	practical, joyful	over-powering, hyper-activity
Yellow	quick, alert mind, sunny, ideas	bright, happy, communicative	egocentric, fearful
Green	caring, empathetic, natural	balance, in harmony, abundant	indecisive, feeling trapped
Blue	peaceful, quiet, introverted	loyal, honest, cooling	depressive, withdrawn
Purple	creative, spiritual, sensitive	powerful, seeker of truth, inspirational	misuse of power, obsessive
Black	feminine energy, mysterious	potential, powerful	identity crisis, hides from the world
White	masculine energy	purity, cleansing	cold, isolating
Brown	earthy, physical	secure, safe	restrictive, barren
Gray	self-reliant, independent	individual, self-sufficient	rigid, critical, uncommunicative
Peach	warm, caring	creative, supportive, charitable, mature	sentimental, low self-esteem
Pink	loving, nurturing, emotional	understanding, sympathetic	immature, needy, emotional, unstable
Turquoise	fresh, sparkling, new ideas	uplifting, refreshing, communicative, cool	cold, isolating
Pastels	softer version of each color	more sensitive, gentle	easily led, impressionable

Our favorite colors can help us understand ourselves better. Everyone has good and bad qualities, strengths and weaknesses. It may be that you have too much of one color energy and too little of another. If you find you are displaying the negative qualities of green, add some red into your life. The positive motivation that red provides will help alleviate your indecisiveness.

Colors for partners and family

When making any decorative changes in your home, make sure you are aware of the color identity and preferences of all the people who will share your home. If one person chooses all the colors, it is very likely that the well-being of other occupants will suffer.

There are cases where a home has been decorated in the colors chosen by one member of the family which clash with the internal colors of another. This can lead to disharmony in the home. There is a strong possibility of arguments and squabbling if the soul colors of the two people are opposite.

To bring balance and harmony into the home where the occupants like contrasting colors, choose a neutral background color. Warm beige, cream, ivory, or any light tint works well. Then introduce a selection of the identity and soul colors in furnishings and accessories such as paintings, cushions, plants, rugs and ornaments.

If there is a room which is generally used by one person more than another, for instance a study, this would be an ideal room to decorate with colors that are harmonious with the soul colors of the user.

Creating a color energy balance

It is a good idea to take one of your soul colors as a starting point for building a color scheme. If, for instance, your soul color is yellow, think of all the different shades of yellow found in nature. There are soft creamy yellow flowers, the golden-yellow of the sun, and deep ochre of the earth. You may decide to use different tones of yellow in different areas in your home or just the one that fits with your tone preference.

Once you have established your main color, choose an object that best represents your color and tone. Imagine this object in its natural setting. If you have chosen a yellow sunflower, create a picture of it surrounded by dark green leaves and rich terracotta earth. This will give you a harmonizing group of colors with which to work.

When decorating a home, remember that you need to create a balance between warm and cool colors. A color scheme that limits you to two or three colors only creates a vibrational imbalance.

If your soul color is blue or green, make sure that you introduce some touches of warm shades, like terracotta or peach, to complement your color scheme. If you are unsure which balancing color to use, the complementary color will always work well. This is the color that is the natural opposing – but balancing – color energy (see the box on page 76).

DEEP BLUE IN A BEDROOM IS EXTREMELY RESTFUL AS IT CALMS AND SOOTHES A RESTLESS OR TIRED MIND AT THE END OF THE DAY.

Using Color for Healing

Every building where we spend a great deal of time should have plenty of air and natural light. Dark, dreary places make us depressed and ill. To be healthy and happy we need the energy from the full spectrum of color vibrations found in natural sunlight. Our lifestyle means that we are constantly receiving an imbalance of colors through our eyes, skin and aura. Even when we go outdoors we often wear tinted sunglasses. Our car windscreens are tinted as well as the window glass in buildings. So we need to identify those colors we require to establish balance. If we do not receive a balance of the seven spectrum colors our metabolism can be seriously affected. Seasonal affective disorder is caused by lack of natural sunlight and you might have symptoms like lethargy, tiredness, moodiness, and depression.

As each color vibration has its own powerful energy and quality we can use certain colors to improve our general state of health or alleviate specific problems.

Light colors in our surroundings raise our vibrations as pale colors reflect more light vitality. Darker colors require more pigment, thus reducing the amount of natural light reflected. So dark and strong colors force a mood on a room. Generally, warm colors are stimulating while cool colors are relaxing. However, you can also have a warm and a cool tone of every color or hue; a dove gray has a warm tone, while steel gray is cool.

When using colors therapeutically, it is best to choose warm colors in rooms where activity is to take place. The living room, dining room, study, television or playroom, workroom, studio, reception area, hall and stairway, are all rooms in which the stimulating qualities of warm colors are appropriate. It is not only the wall coloring that will have an effect on you, but also the colors of blinds, curtains, furnishings, paintings, plants and lights. So check that your house has a variety of color energies.

For rooms where you wish to create a restful and peaceful atmosphere, choose a cool or a pastel color which will emit relaxed, harmonious vibrations. The exact shades will vary according to personal choice, and don't forget that every color has a warm or cold shade.

Living rooms

Living rooms are best decorated in tones relating to the atmosphere you wish to create and to your individual lifestyle. You require one or two main colors, plus a contrasting balancing color. Remember to link these colors to your soul colors. Most living areas are shared by several family members so a neutral background could be the best way to unite all their soul colors.

Kitchens

The healing kitchen is a warm and nurturing place. A place for a gathering, and a place for expressing creativity while nourishing your

body. If you are a working family, it is even more important that your time in the kitchen is enjoyable and it is a place to unwind. The colors in a kitchen can stimulate your senses, releasing the stresses of the day.

Colors for the kitchen are all the earthy colors, rich and warm. Rich nut browns, golden-yellows, terracotta, peach. These need to be set off with lots of green. Green in the kitchen works very well by using plants and herbs, and if this is not possible, then in the crockery and kitchen accessories. White can still be used in the kitchen to give that bright and airy feeling, as long as it is used with lots of color. If you do have a white or neutral kitchen, use bowls of fruit and vegetables to bring color into the room, or hang bunches of dried flowers and herbs from the ceiling, or colorwash your kitchen cupboards

NATURAL EARTHY COLORS BELONG IN A KITCHEN, STIMULATING THE SENSES, WHILE WE NOURISH OUR BODY WITH THE BOUNTY OF THE EARTH.

Dining rooms

The color orange and all colors with orange energy in them are appetite stimulants as well as aiding the digestion. So peaches, apricots and peachy-yellows make the best colors for a dining area and if you eat in the kitchen, having a tablecloth and napkins in these colors will have the same effect.

Bedrooms

If you wish to create a loving, supportive, yet relaxing, bedroom use shades of pink. Pink is a muscle relaxant and the color of love, while

If you wish to find the colors you need for yourself or someone else, for relaxation, support, inspiration and protection, you can always dowse for them using a pendulum (see page 48 for making a pendulum).

Next draw a circle on a piece of white paper. Divide the circle into eight equal segments by drawing a cross and then another cross dissecting the first one. Color each of the segments in a rainbow color. The eighth color could be turquoise or pink.

You first have to understand your pendulum swing. Hold your pendulum out in front of you. Ask it which way it will swing for a 'Yes' answer. Note the direction it swings. Next find out the direction for 'No', and then for 'Unsure, try again.' Once you have determined the pendulum swings, you are ready to begin. The direction will remain constant for you, no matter what other questions you ask later on.

its therapeutic action is reinforced by the color green. Plants are best used to bring green into a pink bedroom, supplemented by green carpeting or rugs, green in the pictures or green bed linen. Pink is a very nurturing and supportive color and pink light filtering through a blind or curtain is emotionally soothing so it can promote a mood of love.

If you wish to create a quiet, cool and peaceful bedroom, you may wish to use blue or green. Blue and green can be cold colors, so take into consideration whether your bedroom gets the morning sun and whether you live in the north or southern hemisphere.

Bathrooms

The bathroom is the most underrated room in the modern house. This can be seen by the fact that bathrooms are often one of the smallest rooms and often found squeezed into a space which cannot be used for any other purpose. The small size of the room, together with the fact that white is a common color choice, makes the bathroom a place where you spend as little time as possible. If you are one of those people who rush in and out of the bathroom, it is likely that you have to learn to care more for your own needs.

We should use the bathroom as a place to relax and nourish the spirit as well as for cleansing purposes. It should be a place in which you want to spend time, caring for yourself. Using color therapy with hydrotherapy (see pages 92-9) in the bathroom can help you replenish lost energy, soothe stress and calm imbalanced emotions.

Choose a color in your bathroom which makes your skin glow. White, gray, blue, black

and avocado green make skin look pale, ill and lifeless. Yellow or orange can make you appear jaundiced and nauseous. Like the bedroom, peach and pink tones reflect a healthy skin glow, and appear warming if you have a cold room. On the other hand, should you want to create a cool, refreshing feel to the bathroom, decorate it with turquoise, blues or greens with white. If this is your preference, make sure that you do not have a fluorescent light fitting, as this type of light is tinted blue, and gives the skin a cold, ghostly appearance. Use an incandescent bulb instead as this is more flattering.

Study or studio

A study needs to be a place which will stimulate the mind but also aid concentration. The choice of colors depends on the type of work you wish to do. If you need a place to study or write, try light tones of blue-green and turquoise. These colors will not distract you from your task and help protect you against stress and eye strain. Turquoise is the color of communication and with golden-yellow, aid clear thinking and effective speaking.

If your work is more of a creative nature, you will need stimulating and inspiring colors. Creamy yellows stimulate mental activity while making a cool room feel warm and cozy. Bright yellow walls can make you feel nauseous, so keep the tone light and fresh.

Children's rooms

Small infants show very soft pastel colors in their auras, and this is why it is traditional to dress babies in these colors. Babies are still very connected to spiritual forces and it is only when the ego develops that they become connected to the earth and material world.

As a child starts to grow and develop he or she becomes increasingly interested in the world about them. Their curiosity and experimental learning can be aided by primaries and other bright colors. But remember that as children develop physically they also develop their own personality and individual qualities. So primary colors may not be suitable for every child.

Many children who have quiet, soft personalities will feel overwhelmed by bright colors, and may withdraw into themselves. These children would greatly benefit from softer but supportive and nurturing colors like warm beige, creams, peaches and pinks. Likewise, older children may need to have quieter, calmer colors in their room if they need to study and concentrate.

Teenagers have always been known to decorate their rooms in colors which are at odds with the family. During the teenage years, a young person has to go through a period of reflection and discover his true self. They have to cast-off the mold of the parents and find their own identity and the colors chosen by young people for their room will reflect this need for self-reflection and identity crisis. It is for this reason that many teenagers choose to wear and decorate with black. Black reflects the need to withdraw within to search for answers. It is only out of the darkness that light can be seen. You will find that after a time, the young person will emerge as a new adult with a new coat of colors and this invariably means that their room will need redecorating again!

Senior citizens

Decorating a room for an elderly relative can play an important part in the harmony of the home and the quality of life that person will enjoy for the rest of their days.

It is so important that the older person has mental stimulation and a reason to get up in the morning. In our latter years it is natural for our thoughts to turn towards spiritual matters, and this can be reflected in color choices. Blues, lavenders, mauves and violet are all color vibrations that connect us to our spiritual side. You can observe this connection when elderly ladies often use lavender water or have a blue hair rinse. Blue, the color of peace, links us to our intuition and higher self, while all forms of violet or purple reflect a desire to develop spiritually.

While the older person may be drawn to these colors, having too much blue or mauve in their room may encourage them to withdraw from this world. This may result in them coping less well with everyday tasks, and losing touch with the physical world.

In your autumn years you can feel a great sense of loneliness and fear, and so loving and supportive colors can be a great comfort. Variety in the colors of the immediate environment can boost interest in the world and stimulate the mind, so using several different, but harmonizing, colors will be of assistance to the elderly. Support these colors with personal belongings and mementoes such as photographs, ornaments, flowers and plants. Make use of aroma and sound (see page 44) and don't forget that wind chimes and bells are soothing and create a reassuring and living sound (see page 59).

DOWSING FOR COLORS (CONT)

Decide which color you wish to find first. If it is the color for relaxation, ask this specific question either in your mind or out aloud. You must be very clear what you are asking, because the pendulum is only a tool which links to your higher mind.

Hold your pendulum directly above the center of your color circle. If it does not swing on its own, start the swing in any direction and the pendulum will correct itself if this is the wrong direction. Once you have found the four colors you need, you may wish to ask the pendulum whether you need a light or dark version of the color, or indeed the pure hue itself. It may mean that you need a pale blue for relaxation, a dark red for inspiration, and a pure purple for protection.

The Fragrant Home

An aromatic home is a tradition long due for revival. The aromas we encounter when entering someone else's home are often subtle and pervasive. They can tell us a great deal about the house and its occupants. Houses where there are children, animals or smokers, all have very distinct smells. Happy homes have different smells from unhappy ones.

Not only does scent affect you emotionally but also physiologically due to the messages that specific odor molecules carry to the brain. People have been quick to use this effect of aroma to their advantage. Some estate agents use the smell of coffee brewing or bread baking to help sell properties, as they know full well how these homely aromas make us feel a particular house is attractive and full of good vibrations. The vibrations we receive through our senses of sight, hearing and smell are so closely linked we often associate sounds with certain colors, while colors invoke particular scents.

Although our sense of smell is the least developed of our senses, our longest lasting memories are often ones linked to aroma. I can remember smells connected with my early childhood, my grandmother's farm and my school had their own, very special, smells.

Odor is a vibration which travels in the ether, thus affecting our etheric body. It is often held in the furnishings and fabric of buildings and, like color vibrations, aromas are absorbed through the etheric body, the skin, as well as the nose. Thus aroma not only affects us physiologically, but also emotionally and mentally. Aromatherapy can be used in many ways to create a natural and protective home environment. It therefore influences the subtle environment. Essential oils have strong disinfecting properties while some are mood enhancing and emote peace and serenity.

Our senses are so closely connected that we can associate aroma with visual color. We prefer the scent of rose, lilac, pine, violet, orange and lemon to things with dark, muddy colors like lard, rubber, olive oil, fish, vinegar or onion.

Our body-odor has only been considered unpleasant since the 18th century and now we have become obsessed by personal hygiene. This has resulted in manufacturers bombarding us with scented toiletries, cosmetics and household products. Unfortunately, most of these scents are made artificially or use extracts of animal scents which are believed to attract the opposite sex.

AROMA INFLUENCES THE SUBTLE ENVIRONMENT WHICH AFFECTS OUR MOODS AND EMOTIONS AND CAN ENHANCE OUR GENERAL WELL-BEING.

Essential Oils

All plants utilize sunlight for their life and growth, locking up life-force energy derived from the sun's rays. If properly preserved, essence from the plant can have a powerful effect on us and our environment. Essential oils are made from the very essence of the plant, and is not just plant material. This life-force element is the reason why real plant essences and oils, rather than those that are artificially made, have beneficial effects.

Essential oils in the home permeate the rooms and fill the ether. We can feed off these nourishing, positive vibrations. Different essential oils create different types of energy and depending on what type of vibrations you feel you need, you can burn one or a mixture of oils.

Essential oils create a pleasant atmosphere when used as a room fragrance. At the same time, specific oils will have an effect on your mood, creating a good ambiance for work, relaxation, inspiration, meditation, romance or sleep. Some oils will help to fumigate the air in cases of disease or illness.

There are several ways in which to use oils for a room fragrance. Add a few drops of

essential oil to a bowl of dried flowers or potpourri. You can also place a few drops of essential oil onto padded clothes hangers and drawer liners. A few drops of oil on a light bulb will be dispersed by the heat. In winter, you can put a couple of drops of essential oil onto a piece of cotton wool which can then be placed behind a radiator. Alternatively, float two drops on a saucer of water positioned close by a warm radiator. This will also act as a humidifier.

There are many different types of essential oil burners which you can buy from shops, but I have found that most of them are badly designed. So, for the best results, look for one with a deep bowl, as the water evaporates very quickly in a shallow one. Also make sure the distance between the bowl and the candle below is not too great, or the flame will never keep the water hot. Here are some oils which can be used for specific purposes although most oils can be used to release aroma into the air.

AROMATIC POTPOURRI CAN REFLECT THE MOOD OF THE ROOM OR THE CHANGING SEASONS.

WHERE TO USE ESSENTIAL OILS (CONT)

For relaxation and sleep use: sandalwood, chamomile, geranium, rose otto, ylang ylang, orange in: bedrooms, bathrooms, therapy rooms.

To clear and purify use: tea tree, lavender, thyme, juniper, eucalyptus, rosemary, lime, pine in: kitchens, utility rooms, treatment and therapy rooms, meditation areas.

For insect deterrent use: lavender, citronella, thyme, peppermint, lemon grass, basil, cinnamon in: all rooms, patio, drawers, cupboards.

For meditation and protection use: sandalwood, frankincense, lavender, cedarwood in: all the house where protection is needed, yoga, relaxation or meditation areas.

Harmonious Scent Vibrations

Aroma is not only a physical force but a spiritual one. Our aura, which is the electro-magnetic force field surrounding all living things, comprises color, sound and aroma. Many different religions realize the significance of odor as reflecting either harmonious or inharmonious vibrations.

A good deal of attention has been focused in recent years on the color vibrations in the aura, although our electromagnetic field is also made up of sounds and aromas. In fact, our sense of smell is the last of our outer senses to be developed, and we need to recapture the auric smell we have lost. It has always been reported that great masters and saints are surrounded by an exquisite scent, while many people have experienced the bad odors permeating people and places where there are bad vibrations.

Bad aromas have often been associated with bad vibrations and psychic forces, which can be found lingering in buildings. Sightings of ghosts and ghostly phenomena are often accompanied by reports of bad odors. Incense made from the resins and barks of various trees such as frankincense, myrrh and sandalwood have been used for centuries to purify the air of any harmful vibrations. Indigenous North Americans used to burn sage in a ceremony known as smudging to purify the mind and body as well as the subtle environment.

When you move into a new home, it is wise to cleanse the air of any lingering bad vibrations by burning some aromatic oils or incense sticks. You could also light a candle which has been scented with lavender or juniper oil.

Here are some ways in which you can make sure that the aromas you use on yourself and in your home are in tune with your own vibrations. Additional recipes are provided in the boxes to the left and right.

Entrance porch or hall

The aroma in your entrance hall will have a special signature as this is where the aromas from all parts of your home mingle. The Japanese place great importance on the vibrations in the entrance hall. This is where you will arrive when you return home and where your visitors will be received. So this area should be a welcoming place where you can spend a few minutes orientating yourself from the outside environment as you move to the one inside.

A few drops of essential oil sprinkled on a doormat gives a special welcome. Bright fresh aromas of citrus oils, like lime, orange, neroli, pettigraine, lemon and bergamot are especially good oils for a hallway. The aromas of these oils are long-lasting and so you can spray the entrance hall and particularly any carpeting in this area with a water spray every day. Often hallways have no windows and so smells can linger there and spread up stairways. Valerie Ann Worwood in her wonderful book *The Fragrant Pharmacy* suggests a mix of lavender and geranium in the hallway.

Add more lavender for the morning, and then more geranium in the afternoon when you want to create a more relaxed and calming atmosphere.

Living rooms

The living room is the main area which collects many different aromas, both from the furnishings and from people. These conflicting scents create a whirlpool or vibrations, each one clashing with another. Aromas in the living room come from chemicals in furniture polish, window cleaners, upholstery and carpet fabrics and from vibrations emitted from people's clothes, as well as their auric scents. To create a harmonious environment where your family and friends can relax and enjoy themselves you need to cleanse these conflicting aromas and instill a new and coordinated mix of scents.

Use essential oils as dynamic fragrances to create different atmospheres in your home. A pottery burner is an economic way to give a subtle aroma and to refresh a room. You can also use a professional diffuser that ionizes the particles it gives off.

If you have an open fireplace, a few drops of essential oil on a log gives off the most positive aromatic vibrations. If you have access to fresh scented herbs like rosemary, lavender or thyme, throw some sprigs onto a coal or charcoal fire. In some places you may be able to obtain wood which has its own scent. Pine or olive branches give off healing and uplifting vibrations as they burn. You can also burn aromatic herbs and branches on a barbecue or in a pizza or bread oven.

Kitchen

The kitchen is the place that we most associate with household smells. The wonderful mixture of natural aroma of fruits, vegetables and herbs can make the kitchen a welcoming and seductive place, but unfortunately it is also the source of many unattractive unwanted and harmful smells.

While cooking food, especially when frying or grilling, tiny particles of fat are released into the atmosphere. These cling to any surfaces with which they come into contact. These molecules lead to greasy work and wall surfaces as well as covering windows and ceilings. Rubbish is another cause of harmful smells and utility rooms which adjoin kitchens often have animal baskets and smells from boots and coats.

To cover and eliminate these smells, modern man has resorted to the use of many chemicals which are just as harmful as the bacteria and smells which they are eradicating. Many people do not realize that they are allergic to many household cleaners and sprays. We take in these chemicals through the air we breathe, through our skins, and by ingesting them from such things as plates and cutlery. These chemicals can cause such problems as asthma, headaches, skin rashes and nausea. Aromatic herbs and oils can

RECIPES FOR NATURAL
CLEANSERS AND AROMAS (CONT)

Clothes freshener: get a handkerchief or small square of natural fiber cloth. Put on 2 drops of three harmonizing essential oils. Place this in a tumble drier with the clothes:
freshening: lavender, rosemary, lemon.
floral: palma-rosa, neroli, geranium.
feminine: jasmine, ylang ylang, vervaine.
masculine: neroli, clary-sage, geranium.

Clothes spray: fill a plant mister with a little water to which you have added a mixture of essential oils and spray it onto the clothes before ironing. Alternatively, put 2 drops of essential oil on a damp cloth and place it over your clothes while ironing. Do not put essential oils directly into your iron, as some oils will leave a residue.

THE HEALING QUALITIES

OF FLOWERS

Red *Rose:* uplifts the spirit, balances masculine and feminine forces within, love and passion. *Chrysanthemum:* for strength and courage and grounding.

Pink *Rose:* unconditional love, healer of the heart. *Carnation:* care and empathy.

Magenta *Foxglove (digitalis):* stabilizes the emotions, caring and nurturing.

Orange *Marigold (calendula):* deep shock from past lives; releases phobias and fears. *Nasturtium:* energizes, anti-depressant.

Yellow *Sunflower:* spiritual container, aids truth and openness. *Daffodil:* optimism, joy, good for nerves, stimulates the mind.

Green *Rosemary:* guardian and protector.

Blue *Cornflower, forget-me-not:* peace-bringer, holds past memories. *Bluebell, blue iris:* purify the atmosphere. *Hyacinth:* lifts vibrations, inspirational.

Indigo/violet *Pansy, violet, lilac, lavender:* all have healing energies which cleanse the atmosphere.

White *Rose, lily, white orchid:* cleansing, purity and protection.

make effective and environmentally friendly cleansers, toners and moisturizers.

It is wise to cleanse dining areas, without creating strong scent vibrations. Try to keep chemical aromas well away from dining rooms as these may put you off your food and impair the appetite. Rather, let the natural aroma of fresh herbs and spices act as nourishing vibrations in eating areas.

Bedrooms and bathrooms

The bedroom and bathroom should not only be a place where you can retire to sleep, they should be a nourishing place where you can enjoy time, relaxing and caring for yourself. You can clean negative vibrations from a bedroom with aroma in the same ways as suggested for the living areas. A drop of essential oil on a pillow can help you relax as you drift off to sleep. Cupboards and drawers can have scented sachets and lining papers. Burning romantic and relaxing oils in a room burner will instill your bedroom with loving and healing vibrations. You may wish to practice some form of relaxation technique or meditation in your bedroom. If you do, burn essential oils which will help still the mind and help you connect with your higher self, so harmonizing the different aspects of your being.

After you have cleaned surfaces and the toilet bowl in the bathroom with natural cleaners, you can make the bathroom a place where you can release the tension of the day. In *The Fragrant Pharmacy*, Valerie Ann Worwood suggests you put a couple of drops of essential oil on the cardboard inside a roll of toilet paper. The cardboard will soak up the aroma and release it gradually over a period of time. A bowl containing potpourri is a colorful and healthy way of keeping your bathroom smelling fresh and clean. You do have to remember to add oils and toss the potpourri like a salad when the aroma starts to fade.

The bathroom provides the perfect setting for a collection of candlesticks or a candelabra. Having a bath by candlelight provides both a relaxing atmosphere, and also allows your eyes a rest from harsh artificial lighting. Use scented candles or place a couple of drops of essential oils on the candle taking care not to wet the wick. Aromatic oils used in the bath permeate the skin and can be either stimulating, releasing or relaxing. You can also add certain essential oils to body lotions, face and hand creams and to vegetable oils which are used for massage.

Flowers for protection

Flowers create a peaceful and harmonious environment. They can protect and inspire, too, so use them for visualization, meditation or as a gift for someone you care about (see box, left). They carry with them certain messages, depending on their type, color and aroma. When you understand the meaning of flowers, you can really use these gifts of nature to enhance the quality of your life. When selecting flowers to buy or grow in your garden think carefully about their healing qualities, too.

FLOWERS CARRY WITH THEM CERTAIN MESSAGES. WHEN YOU UNDERSTAND THE MEANING OF FLOWERS, USE THEM TO ENHANCE YOUR LIFE.

Hydrotherapy

Since early times, water has been known to have healing and therapeutic qualities. Water is the essence of life. It is a particularly good conductor of electricity, but there are many energies carried in water. Due to its capacity to cleanse and purify electromagnetic vibrations, water has been used symbolically to cleanse the human mind and spirit. People still bathe in holy rivers; use water for baptism and drink spa water for its healing properties.

Water is a natural element which has a strong effect on our home and personal environment. Our body is made up of 60 per cent water and our brain of 90 per cent water, so is it any wonder water plays such an important part in our life. Our homes too are affected by water. The water in the ground under a building can create energy imbalances which will affect our health and quality of life.

Hydrotherapy makes use of the electrical properties of water to improve the electromagnetic balance in your body. This increases the electrical charge of the body's cells, which in turn stimulates the body's systems into activity. There are many ways water can be of benefit to us. It can stimulate and relax and help relieve and heal a host of ailments. It can also purify the subtle atmosphere of a room. To use water effectively to improve health and the quality of life, you need to provide a comfortable and well-designed space in which you can enjoy the benefits.

BATHING IS ALWAYS ENHANCED BY BEING LINKED TO NATURE AND THE BATHROOM SHOULD BE AS LIGHT AND AIRY AS POSSIBLE.

The Lost Art of Bathing

SAVING WATER

Highly industrial nations consume a vast amount of water. Individual families of four in the United States of America consume an average of 220 gallons (1000 liters) per day. We do need to take responsibility for our use of this precious commodity and prevent further contamination. Here are a few tips to achieve this:

✍ Only use the washing machine with a full load.

✍ Wash up once a day.

✍ Do not wash your car with a garden hose.

✍ Get a low flush cistern for your toilet.

✍ Use a watering can to water your garden.

✍ Alternate a shower with your bath.

✍ Fix leaks and dripping taps.

✍ Use only biodegradable and ecofriendly cleaners.

It is only during the last century that bathing became a private affair. For centuries, bathing was an essential part of social life, an activity central to the fabric of society. The baths were an important meeting place, a social center for relaxation and debate. At the same time you were performing the bathing ritual, you could be massaged and pampered. The baths were a place where you could both exercise or rest, a recreation complex at its best. Due to the constraints of having to go to a public place to bathe, one didn't go every day, and it was only relatively recently that bathing was brought to the home, where it could be performed more often.

Bathing has remained a solitary pursuit during the last century. In fact, the Victorians, who developed sophisticated hot water and plumbing systems, still held the attitude that one bathed out of necessity and for hygienic purposes only. This sentiment still perpetuates today, and the bathroom is mostly confined to being the smallest and darkest room.

Bathing today is still, for the most part, a clinical affair. We scrub away our natural body oils and odors, and our skin's protective covering. We then replace our lost oils with body lotions and perfumes concocted from the glands of other animals.

Bathing should be restored to its rightful place as both a pleasurable and relaxed activity, which can be enjoyed either alone or in a group. Often it is the only time we have to ourselves in the day, so we should make the most of it in an environment which offers us the best opportunity to de-stress. Bathing should be a celebration of the human form. Perfumes, oils massaged into the skin, work towards keeping your body supple, youthful and sweet-smelling.

Once we realize we do not have to lock ourselves away in a small, dark room, we can incorporate bathing spaces into the heart of our home. Baths do not have to be housed in bathrooms. They can be part of a bedroom, part of a loft or cellar. As water is one of the four natural elements it has a strong connection with the other three; earth, air and fire. So a place of bathing can be enhanced by linking it to nature by opening to a courtyard and garden or sky. I once saw a flat in London where the bathroom led off a first-floor bedroom down some steps. The bath commanded a stunning view over the garden and neighboring countryside. It was a place where you could take a book or magazine. You could also spend time paying attention to your toiletries or chatting to a friend over a glass of wine.

Home water supply

The quality of the water we consume in the home has a direct bearing on the quality of life we will enjoy. So much ground water has become contaminated through toxic sprays and chemicals used on the land that we have almost forgotten the healing qualities of water. Metal compounds also leak into our drinking water from industry and old lead

When you move house you may sense an unhappy atmosphere in your new home. Water will help you cleanse the place of any lingering emotional or psychic vibrations. This simple ceremony can also be used to clean a room which has been closed up for some time. The pine essential oil cleanses the air so you can breathe more easily, while frankincense frees trapped ch'i and promotes the cleansing properties of the water.

Make sure you have a glass bowl of pure water. You may like to place into the water two drops of frankincense and two drops of pine essential oil. Pray for happiness in love and family life and ask that your home be cleansed from all harmful and impure vibrations. Dip two fingers into the bowl and flick the blessed water around the room. You can move from room to room performing this purification ceremony.

pipes so it is virtually impossible to get pure drinking water from our water supply.

It is now up to us to make sure we can enjoy pure water. Water filtering is the safest way of obtaining pure water and there are various products available which do this. The easiest way to have pure water for drinking is to buy a water filter system. This could be a jug or a filter system which fits directly into

INCORPORATE A BATH INTO YOUR BEDROOM AND MAKE IT A PLACE WHERE YOU CAN LINGER AND PAMPER YOURSELF.

your cold water inlet pipe. There are other types available which fit snugly over a tap. These filtering systems take out harmful chemicals and minerals and improve the taste and the smell of the water.

Creating a Home Health Spa

MAKING YOUR HOME HEALTH SPA

✎ Keep a candlestick or candles permanently in the bathroom.

✎ Use soft lighting, especially bulbs with a yellow or pinkish tint.

✎ Keep moisture- loving plants in the room.

✎ Make sure you have a portable radio or tape available to play relaxing music.

✎ Use a cotton bath mat, flannel and towels.

✎ Try a natural bristle back brush, loofah or sisal or hemp friction glove.

✎ Vegetable oil soaps made with natural plant extracts are aromatic and leave your skin silky smooth.

✎ Natural shampoo, conditioners made from chamomile, rosemary or henna strengthen the hair and enhance its color and texture.

Rather than think of the bathroom as a place to clean your body, create your own health spa at home so that it includes a variety of relaxation aids such as sound, color, light, air and moisture-loving plants.

When choosing a bath it does not have to be the standard size. You can also get oval and corner tubs and those with a built-in seat. Shorter but wider baths allow you to have a deep soak without the water getting so cold. If you have a larger oval bath you can easily share your bathing time with other members of the family. If you are worried that this is unhygienic, take a lesson from the Japanese method of bathing. First have a shower during which you can soap and scrub your body. This thoroughly cleanses the body before getting into the bath. Bathing together as a family can provide a wonderful time for relaxation and this intimate time will bring the family together.

Showers

So many bathrooms are fitted with showers that do not work properly that it is no wonder people have resisted showering for so long. . A shower needs to be big enough for you to move around without knocking your elbows when washing your hair. It also needs to have a good strong pressure which keeps the water at an ambient temperature. Try to purchase a quality shower head with a pulsating and jet spray. This will enable you to have a massage on your shoulders and back. Remember peo-

MAKING YOUR HOME HEALTH SPA (CONT)

❧ Buy a herbal toothpaste and natural toothbrush.

❧ Clean the bath with a mixture of either vinegar or lemon juice and water.

❧ Use potpourri or natural herbal spray as a room deodorizer.

❧ Moisturize your skin with natural moisturizer.

❧ Have a chair or stool in your bathroom so you can enjoy a manicure or pedicure.

❧ Get as much natural light and air into the room as possible, keeping a healthy atmosphere in the bathroom.

PLACE CANDLES IN FRONT OF A MIRROR TO DOUBLE THE STARRY EFFECT.

VISUALIZATION THEMES WHILE
IN A SHOWER, BATH OR
FLOATATION TANK

✍ Imagine you are standing under a waterfall and let the crystal water droplets pour down onto you and through you. Feel it cleansing and refreshing every part of you.

✍ Visualize yourself standing over a fountain which is the fountain of life. Imagine the water rising up through you from the base of your spine and out of the top of your head. It recharges and fills you with new life.

✍ See yourself floating in the ocean and that your breath is connected to the rise and fall of the waves. Your hands and legs are stretched out in the shape of a starfish and your hair trails out behind you. Feel yourself relaxing more and more as you drift upon the water.

ple are different heights, so having a shower fixed at one particular height may be all right for one person but not for another.

If your water tank is not above ceiling height or is in the ceiling directly above you, your shower may need an electric booster to help with the pressure. Check where your tank is before installing a shower to make sure you have enough water pressure.

Flotation tank

Deep relaxation can be achieved by suspending yourself in a watery environment. This resembles the embryonic fluid of the womb and connects you to your own body fluid.

You can make a simulated flotation tank at home very easily by mixing an Epsom salt and sea salt bath at body temperature. Use an eye mask and have some restful music playing in the background. In this way you will come close to a commercial flotation tank without feeling claustrophobic or having to leave the safety of your home environment.

Into a bath or water at body temperature add 1 lb (500 g) of Epsom salts, ½ lb (250 g) of sea salt and 1 dessert spoon of clear iodine (so it does not stain the bath). Lie in the bath for 20 minutes, topping up with hot water as you require.

Turkish bath

The ancient custom of Turkish bathing is based on the progression from hot to warm to cold chambers, finishing with a body shampoo and a warm shower which is gradually turned cold. Alternatively, a plunge into a cold pool finishes off the bath, leaving you

refreshed and invigorated. It is difficult to provide several rooms to experience a Turkish-style bath, but the principles can be incorporated into your bathing sequence.

Sauna

The sauna has been used for centuries in many Scandinavian and Austrian homes to combine physical revival with mental relaxation. The sauna has now taken over as the favorite way of cleansing the skin by heat. The combination of free perspiration and rapid cooling stimulates the liver and circulation, reduces the amount of muscular and nervous tension and heightens mental awareness.

The traditional sauna is a log cabin lined with pine boards and heated by an electric or gas stove. Lying on top of the stove are several hard rocks, made of peridotite, a granite that can withstand extreme temperatures. By ladling water on to these rocks periodically the hot dry air is converted to moist air. Experts claim that the sudden ionization of the air by water produces maximum benefit. Try adding essential oils to the water before you put on the heat source as these will enter the body through inhalation and are excellent cleansers and detoxifiers. Mix 2 drops of eucalyptus, tea tree or pine essential oils per pint (600 ml) of water. These oils will leave the body by perspiration through the skin.

Do not stay in a sauna too long, but alternate short spells with a cool shower in a nearby room. If you have a heart or respiratory problem you should not take a sauna, but for the healthy it is most enjoyable. Any temporary weight loss should be replaced by drinking fluid and having a light, salty snack.

You should not take a sauna for at least two hours after a meal as this will strain the heart.

For the simple reason that the sauna involves a heating-cooling-rest process, most saunas are installed near to, or designed to include, a dressing room and shower. A sauna can be rectangular or square to allow for maximum use of bench space, but octagonal, round or wedge-shaped saunas aren't unknown. Fortunately, it is not necessary to have a picturesque setting for a sauna and you will still be able to enjoy its invigorating benefits if it is housed in an outside storeroom, barn or corner of a basement. Most of us are not lucky enough to have the space and be able to afford the cost of installing a sauna at home, but we can always go along to a local health club for this treat.

Whirlpool or jacuzzi

Whirlpools are expensive to buy and run, although they are a good aid when creating a home health spa. The water is passed through pressurized jets and when the water is mixed with air this provides a very fine water massage. Try to immerse yourself at a temperature of 95-104°F (35-40°C) as this gives a sense of buoyancy. Jacuzzis are an excellent way of reducing stress and stimulating the flow of blood into the muscles. Add three drops of your favorite essential oil to the water. Close your eyes and use a creative visualization while you relax in your jacuzzi or hot tub.

THIS LARGE, OLD-FASHIONED BATH TUB IS THE PERFECT PLACE TO SOAK AWAY STRESS WHILE DOING A RELAXING VISUALIZATION.

The Lighthouse

Light is the purest healing force in the Universe, for pure sunlight contains all the elements necessary to keep every living thing in perfect health. The life-giving force of white sunlight needs to circulate freely through us, linking us to the cosmic forces. Blockage of this energy results in a state of disharmony or 'disease'. When this happens, we need to restore the balance of this radiant energy, allowing it to flow freely again.

Just as we need a varied and balanced diet if we are to stay healthy, so too do we need a balance of the seven spectrum colors. These travel in vibrations and we pick them up through our eyes and our skin and energy field (aura).

It has been said that life in the light is necessary for both biological and physiological health. On a physical level, the pituitary gland, and on the spiritual level, the soul, both need to be nurtured by living light. Not only do we need this energy, but our ability to absorb and utilize it will affect our quality of life. When we have the ability to do this well, we glow with good health and have tons of energy.

Light and air are our primary sources of ch'i and the vital energy we absorb from light helps us to pass through the ups and downs of life without signs of strain or stress. The ability to absorb and utilize life-force energy also creates a strong immune system which resists disease and other harmful vibrations that surround us.

If we live in an environment which offers us little opportunity to absorb ch'i from light and air we will operate at half our optimum level. Our brain will be dull and fuzzy, we will suffer from a poor memory and find it hard to think clearly or make decisions. Emotionally we will feel drained and depressed without knowing why. Physically, we will suffer from fatigue and recurrent viral and bacterial infections.

Our home environment can greatly influence our ability to absorb vital energy into our system and so directly affect our well-being and quality of life. So it is essential we pay attention to the light and air in our home if we are to improve our health and lifestyle.

Nowadays we spend 90 per cent of our life indoors. Our homes and offices have artificial lights, and even when we go outdoors, we often wear tinted sunglasses and then we spend a great deal of time in a car behind a colored windshield. If we receive only certain colors in the spectrum into our system, we will find the deficiency of certain wavelengths results in many mental, emotional and physical problems. Nervous fatigue, eye strain, irritability, hyperactivity, lack of concentration and a lowered immune system can all result from lack of exposure to full-spectrum light.

Everyone feels the immediate benefits of being in a light and airy environment. Natural light influences the pituitary and pineal glands, both master glands of our endocrine system. These control the release of normalizing and desirable hormones into the body, which are closely linked to our moods and emotions.

We all need a minimum of 30 minutes a day exposed to natural daylight without screens or sunglasses. In the home you can bring in more daylight by opening a window. If this is not possible, in winter for example, it is essential that you install full-spectrum lighting. Fluorescent or striplights have a blue bias, while common incandescent bulbs have a yellowish tint. This means that the other color vibrations are greatly diminished, causing energy imbalances in our system.

LIGHT IS NOT ONLY ESSENTIAL TO OUR BODY, BUT FEEDS AND UPLIFTS OUR SPIRITS.

Artificial Light

COMBINE DIFFERENT TYPES OF LIGHTING IN ONE ROOM FOR YOUR CHANGING NEEDS AND MOODS.

Seasonal affective disorder (SAD) has now been identified as one of the main causes of many sleep and emotional problems. Depressive symptoms can be significantly improved within two to four days when a person is exposed to full-spectrum lighting. Bright artificial light has also been successfully used in the treatment of premenstrual syndrome as well as seasonal bulimia and other eating disorders.

When researchers first worked on SAD and light therapy they realized that the problem was the absence of daylight. The answer was to copy daylight as exactly as possible by using special lamps which not only give off good-quality, visible light, but also emit a small amount of ultra violet (UV) radiation, about the same as normal sunlight. The energy from these specially designed lamps ensures an even spread of colors and is not as patchy as normal fluorescent tubes. It has since been found that the ultra violet light is not necessary to balance the color energies and for caution's sake is avoided in modern full-spectrum lamps.

Light has different qualities, depending on the weather, season, time of day and location. It can be direct, reflected or diffused and the brightness and quality of the light will create different moods and atmosphere. We can reproduce these different types of light artificially and they each have a strong effect on our interaction with rooms in our home.

Direct light is needed when we have to do a task requiring precision and concentration. Reading, writing, drawing, painting or sewing are all activities that require bright, concentrated light.

Reflected light is suitable in a room where you need an even distribution of light. Light can be bounced off walls and ceilings, to give a softer light, or in a dark or small room you can use mirrors to greatly increase the general level of light in the room. When we require good general lighting but also need areas of bright light, reflected and direct lighting works together to give a good harmonious and functional light to a room.

Filtered natural daylight creates a gentle, quiet feeling. We often experience filtered light through blinds and shutters. We can also create filtered light through fine fabrics, screens, shutters, frosted or colored glass. Filtered light is especially useful in bedrooms, treatment rooms for therapists, relaxation areas and bathrooms.

Pinpoint focus of a beam of light can be used to highlight certain objects in a room. A picture, sculpture, flower arrangement, plant or special piece of furniture would benefit from accent lighting. You have to remember that spotlights give off heat, so always place the light away from anything which could be damaged or is flammable.

In his book *The Natural House*, David Pearson recommends the best locations for rooms so that they maximize sunlight. The bedrooms should be orientated towards the sunrise. This puts us in touch with the natural cycle of day and night, so that we wake up with the sun.

LIGHT IN THE HOME

No form of artificial lighting can match the wonders of natural sunlight, so we must try to allow light and air to come into our home from outside.

☞ Keep windows clean and check that they all open.

☞ Draw curtains back as far as possible and keep blinds up during the day.

☞ Move away any plants or objects which obstruct light coming into your home.

☞ Use mirrors opposite windows in rooms with low light levels.

☞ Use low-energy lighting or full-spectrum lights where possible.

☞ Create skylights, atriums and sunrooms where you can, so that you can enjoy the benefits of sunlight.

People who find it difficult to wake up in the morning should make sure that they have curtains or blinds made from lightweight or sheer fabrics so that they respond to the early morning light. Sunlight wakes us up naturally, in tune with nature.

Breakfast rooms should also face the early morning sun, so that you can enjoy your first meal in natural daylight. This ensures your activities are synchronized with your biorhythms. Kitchens, living rooms and play areas should be located where they can make the most of late morning and afternoon sunshine. Offices benefit from daylight during the middle of the day, while studies which are used in the evening after work can be located on the darker side of the house. Storage areas, larders and garages are best located away from the sun. If you are planning on adding these to the main house, they will provide extra insulation if located on the cold side of the house.

Until recently, artificial light has given off a radiance which is biased to a particular color range in the spectrum. This means that it is not giving off balanced vibrations, and being in a room which is constantly lit by such a light can result in problems such as headaches, eye-strain, loss of energy, nausea and even fits.

Incandescent bulbs, which are ordinary household bulbs, give off much more red light than normal daylight. This is why these lamps appear yellow when lit and make the colors in the room more yellowy than normal. In fact, most lights produce more infrared heat than they do light.

Fluorescent bulbs, on the other hand, give off ultraviolet and blue light. These lights also send out pulsing vibrations and though you may not notice this at first, older lights often start to hum and flicker. This means they can interfere with our own vibrations, setting up a resonance within us, which can make us hyperactive and irritable. Fluorescent strip lights can also adversely affect your eye-sight and people who work under these lights often suffer from sore eyes. The blue coloring can make you feel cold and all the colors in the room will take on a bluish tinge. A new generation of compact fluorescent lamps are now available which are much more efficient and longer lasting than the older type. They cut down on heat production so do not attract as much dust and pollution as other types of bulbs may do.

Tungsten-halogen lamps give a bright, white light close to daylight in quality. These are powerful lights and are good for general illumination. Low-voltage lights are more energy efficient and are perfect for spot lighting and accent lighting. Both these types of lights are expensive, but the bulbs have an extremely long life and can ultimately save on energy costs.

Full-spectrum lamps, which more closely resemble a balance of spectral light found in daylight, are now being produced. The new generation bulbs are far healthier than the originals as they improve mood and performance and have no long-term side effects, like other artificial lights. Unfortunately, full-spectrum lights can increase the levels of ultra-violet radiation in a room, especially where electrical equipment such as a computer or microwave is used. In these cases, you will have to take measures to combat the build-up of positive ions.

Therapeutic Lighting

There are times when we need the benefits and qualities of a particular color light.

Colored light bulbs

These can be used in a number of situations in our home to balance problems we may have, and aid healing processes.

Blue light
Blue light helps us sleep and calms the mind. It is not a good idea, however, to use it for reading by as blue light can strain the eyes. A blue light next to the bed can help calm hyperactive children and is useful for soothing childhood diseases like chickenpox or where the symptoms include a high temperature and hot or itchy skin rashes.

Green light
The benefits of green light are greatest when you have your eyes closed. Use green light to relax and unwind, especially after a hot bath or when you practice a relaxation technique. Green candles with added drops of essential oil are ideal for calming and balancing the emotions. Green light speeds up the body's own healing mechanism: good for recuperation.

Orange light
Use orange light to combat depression and lift your mood. Orange light in a living room creates a friendly and communicative atmosphere and orange candles or side-lights in the dining room stimulate the appetite and create a warm, intimate atmosphere. In a bedroom, orange will be stimulating so should be avoided if you suffer from insomnia.

Pink light
This is particularly useful in the bedroom, and can be used in table lamps where a loving and nurturing environment is needed. Pink light is especially useful when you are feeling lonely, unloved, or grieving.

Red light
The wavelength of the color red has an arousing effect, preparing us to respond to danger. Recently, a red environment was created in a football team's dressing room to stimulate the players before a match.

If you want to give your bedroom that exotic and alluring atmosphere, use a red bulb in your bedside light. Red is also an excellent color to use in a cold room, or when there is insufficient heating in winter.

Violet light
Violet light has been used successfully in many mental institutions to help people with obsessive behavior patterns and neuroses. The frequency of the violet vibration activates the pineal gland which produces endorphins (chemicals found in the brain) that have a calming and uplifting effect. At home, it can aid meditation by balancing the sides of the brain. Only use violet light for short periods of time for specific balancing treatments.

COLORED LIGHTS

✍ Blue light is exceptionally soothing and cooling. Use it in hot rooms, or when you are suffering from anger or a fever.

✍ Green light is very cooling and soothing but is not recommended when you wish to read or concentrate on a task.

✍ Orange light is warming and stimulating. It creates an atmosphere of happiness and vitality.

✍ Pink light has muscle relaxing qualities. It is also a gently warming and loving color.

✍ Red light is physically warming and emotionally arousing, so it is also associated with sexual passion.

✍ Violet light bulbs can help harmonize your mental and emotional state.

The Breathing Home

Our home is an extension of ourselves and, like us, needs to breathe. Fresh air and natural light must flow freely through the home if the occupants are to enjoy bountiful energy and good health. If we live in a building which remains sealed most of the year it is like living in a plastic bag and we end up breathing in dirt and filth.

If you want to make the most of the protection and love your home can offer, you must allow it to breathe. To create a warm, dry and healthy atmosphere indoors, moisture and toxins need to be carried to the outside of the house. Not only do physical elements need to be eliminated, but bad energetic vibrations can also be dispelled in this way.

Old buildings will usually function effectively if allowed to work as they were intended. If there is an impervious outer layer to your home, moisture will not be able to pass through the building and evaporate from the surface. If mortars, plasters, renders and finishes of a permeable kind are used, moisture can pass through them and the interior of the building is kept dry and warm. So if moisture is prevented from evaporating on the outside, it will move to the inner walls where it will evaporate into the room. This lowers the temperature inside, making the room damp and unhealthy.

If your interior walls are also painted with impermeable materials the moisture will become trapped within the wall. In hot weather, moisture behind the paint will vaporize, causing blistering, and in cold weather, the wall surface may be damaged by frost action. If dense plasters have been used for rendering, gradual increase in salt concentrations within the wall will tend to blow the surface off the wall or worse still lead to expansion of the plaster itself with consequent bulging.

As long as there is a good damp course, a modern house can also benefit from the use of natural breathable materials. By allowing air and moisture to leave woodwork in walls, timbers will be less likely to succumb to wet or dry rot. Using a lime-based mortar, which is weaker than the building material it covers, allows water to escape naturally from stone or brickwork which would otherwise rapidly decay.

ONLY FRESH AIR CAN MAKE US FEEL ALIVE, SPARKLING AND ENERGETIC. SEA AIR IS FULL OF NEGATIVE IONS WHICH HELP CALM AND RELAX US.

Breathing Life into Your Home

INDOOR POLLUTION

Everyone should be aware of the sources of indoor air pollution. These include:

☞ Tobacco smoke.

☞ Aerosols and sprays (including perfumes).

☞ Gas or smoke fumes from cookers and fires.

☞ Chemicals emitted by synthetic carpets, curtains and furniture.

☞ Plastics.

☞ Polyurethane foam, including foam carpet underlay.

☞ Oil tanks, petrol and detergents.

☞ Certain bricks, cements and aggregates.

☞ Ground water.

☞ Natural gas.

☞ Chemically-made paints and varnishes.

Conservationists have worked out that to replace the oxygen breathed by one person we need approximately 1½ sq yd (m) of grass or 5 yd (m) of green leaves, so it is in our own interests to preserve and replenish the fast diminishing reserve of trees on earth.

Only fresh air can make us feel fresh, sparkling and energetic and by learning to breathe properly can we learn to heal ourselves and enjoy life to the full. The deep breath provides nourishment for both the body and the mind. Air is the primary source of life energy and you can direct it to any part of your body, or you can direct it to protect your home and belongings.

Some polluting items can be removed from your home altogether, while others, such as sprays and smoking, can be avoided. Checking ground and water pollution requires the services of an expert or you can dowse for problems yourself (see page 48). People are also the source of pollution as our bodies produce a number of toxins, such as acetone, ethyl alcohol and methyl alcohol.

Plant protection

Plants do more than just brighten up our home or work environment. They also make our environment a healthier place and can even help us avoid catching a cold. Dr Wolverton, who worked for many years as a researcher at NASA, studied how air pollution levels can build up in a confined space and helped develop techniques for clearing them.

Although many people do not suffer visible ill-effects from the polluted environment, some do develop allergies, headaches, asthma and congestion. These problems tend to get worse during winter when the air is naturally drier. This dryness is compounded by central heating and air conditioning. Our mucous membranes become irritated by the dryness, making us more susceptible to colds.

Plants emit moisture and so can help to counteract dryness in the atmosphere. By bringing more plants inside we can all breathe more easily. Formaldehyde is the most commonly found toxin in indoor air and can be found in resins, paper towels, tissues, floor coverings, fabrics, garbage bags, chipboard and plywood. Plants are particularly good at removing formaldehyde from the atmosphere and certain varieties of plants are better at doing this than others. The following were found by Dr Wolverton to be particularly good at removing toxins from the air:

Peace lily (Spathiphyllum)
Chrysanthemum morifolium
Gerbera daisy (*Gerbera jamesonii*)
Bamboo palm (*Chamaedorea seifrizii*)
Dwarf date palm (*Phoenix roebelenii*)
Moth orchid (Phalaenopsis)
English ivy (*Hedera helix*)
Philodendron (Philodendron)

PLANTS CLEANSE AND PURIFY STALE AIR AS WELL AS
ABSORBING SOUND. USE THEM TO CREATE A
RELAXING AND INTIMATE CORNER.

COMBATING INDOOR AIR POLLUTION IN YOUR HOME

≈ Do not smoke or allow smokers in your home.

≈ Get your chimney cleaned regularly.

≈ Open windows at different sides of the home to create cross ventilation.

≈ Seal cracks in floor edges, pipes and walls, especially in basements.

≈ Use extractor fans to expel any dampness.

≈ Buy an air-filter to clean the dust and bacteria.

≈ Use an ionizer to create negative ions.

≈ Use porous paints and wall coverings.

≈ Place an air vent in your roof so fumes can leave your home.

≈ Have extractor fans in bathrooms and kitchens, if they have no windows.

REDUCING POSITIVE IONS

☞ Keep electrical equipment away from your bed.

☞ Use less electrical equipment.

☞ Try to keep food in a larder or if possible buy a new CFC-free refrigerator.

☞ Keep a comfortable indoor humidity by ventilating to the outside.

☞ Use a protective radiation screen over your VDU and wear protective glasses.

☞ Learn deep yogic breathing.

☞ Check that you have comfortable and supportive chairs so you can breathe more easily.

☞ Burn cleansing and purifying aromatic oils.

☞ Dry your hair naturally.

☞ Use a pressure cooker instead of a microwave.

☞ Get an ionizer.

Choose low-maintenance plants such as those that do not need a lot of natural light or constant watering. You can minimize problems which are caused by the build-up and circulation of mold spores by avoiding compost. Instead, use expanded clay granules.

Positive and negative ions

Like batteries, our bodies contain positive and negative polarities. These polarities affect our electrical currents and can create confusion in the mind and body if there is an excessive build up of either charge.

Research has shown that in houses where air-conditioning and central heating become ion-depleted, the result is tiredness, and loss of mental and physical efficiency. Electrical wiring and appliances in the home can contribute to a build-up of positively charged ions and emit various forms of radiation, both of which affect the quality of the air in your home. Many buildings have radiation 25 times that found in the external environment.

Electrical appliances like televisions, microwave ovens, hair dryers and refrigerators all emit hazardous pollutants and contribute to the formation of positive ions. When too many positive ions occur, you may become tense, irritable and uneasy in the same way as before a thunder storm. The effects of drowsiness, irritation, nausea and fatigue are similar to those experienced from being in a crowded, airless room.

An ionizer filters out dirt and dust particles from the air as well as emitting negative ions into the atmosphere. If you do not wish to buy a commercially produced ionizer, you can use a natural quartz crystal instead.

Quartz crystals contain silicon dioxide which imbues them with pyro-electrical qualities. This means that, when stimulated, they emit electrical impulses giving the crystal the capacity to absorb, store and release vibrations. A crystal is also able to restore balance between positive and negative charges. Manmade crystals are used in communication technology today in the form of the silicon chip. Just as a computer needs software before it can be of any use, so you have to program your crystal.

Quartz crystals come in a variety of colors and sizes and are extremely beautiful. They can be single crystals or in the form of a cluster. You can select either clear quartz, amethyst, or smoky quartz for your ionizer. Once you have the crystal you will need to cleanse it of any negative vibrations it already holds. To do this, place it in the sunlight for some hours. Alternatively, you can wash it in sea water or salt water. If this is not possible, pass it under a running tap for ten minutes or so. The length of time will have to be decided by you, using your intuition.

Now your crystal is ready to be programmed. Think very clearly what you wish the crystal to do. Place it in your right hand, or if it is a large crystal cluster, hold your right hand palm down over it. Now think or say the words, 'I program this crystal to balance and heal.'

Place your crystal on a table in the room you wish to clear. You can put a programmed crystal on a microwave, computer or television, or any object causing electronic smog.

TO REDUCE INDOOR POLLUTION, REGULARLY CHECK YOUR CHIMNEY FOR CRACKS AND CLEAN IT.

The Spiritual Home

A house can be healthy but still lack the spirit of the home we need. To enjoy true well-being, our home should offer us physical comfort, have a loving atmosphere, and also be a sacred space where we can spend time nurturing our spiritual aspirations.

Real security comes from a feeling of belonging, and our home can help us to find our true place in the world. If we consciously create a healing home, it will help us to find our spiritual connections with nature, the community and the planet, while providing us with a safe haven where we can enjoy inner peace and contentment. Our home can be the means by which we create a balance between these external and internal systems. We can then live in harmony with ourselves and all life.

If you have a home that helps you link to the spiritual side of your being, it will be permeated with loving and protective energy. Each of us needs to have a mystical place of our own. If you do not know of one of these places in your area, create a sacred place in your home. This may be a place for prayer, relaxation and contemplation, or somewhere in which to meditate.

Whether you have a particular spiritual belief or not, it has been proved that we can all benefit from spending ten minutes a day in contemplation. Meditation relaxes and calms our mind which is over-active during the day. Modern living has brainwashed us into believing that we should work flat out all year round, instead of following the natural energy rhythms of the seasons. This means that most people suffer from stress and have forgotten how to truly relax. The healing home can help us relax and unwind, so that we can conserve and renew our energy needs.

A meditation space needs to be a quiet and tranquil part of your home. If you do not have a room which you could convert to a relaxation area, your bedroom probably has the right mood for meditation. A garden and nature has very healing and relaxing vibrations, so in warm weather, a verandah, balcony or terrace is an ideal place to practice meditation.

THIS SECLUDED HAMMOCK PROVIDES THE PERFECT PLACE TO RENEW YOUR ENERGY LEVELS
AND PONDER ON THE MEANING OF LIFE.

Here are some ideas for ways in which you can enhance the vibrations in and around your home.

Protective light

☞ Use your thought vibrations to protect your house with light. Every time you go out, visualize your home circled with a protective white or violet light. This will provide a sheath of protection.

☞ Do this at night, too, when you go to bed, so that you and your family can rest peacefully through the night.

Color protection

☞ The North American Indians used to hang a piece of turquoise over their doorways and today continue the tradition by painting their door frames with turquoise paint which absorb bad vibrations before they can enter the dwelling.

☞ In Japan, flags and banners are erected from poles, or hung from doorways or trees to keep away bad vibrations. You can write a prayer on each piece of cloth asking for protection of a certain part of your home and its occupants.

Creating a Relaxation Room

Some people meditate while sitting upright on a chair, others prefer to lie down. Unfortunately, if you lie down, you run the risk of falling asleep. It is therefore best to have a meditation cushion or stool on which to sit. Keep this seat for meditation only, although you will probably find that your pet or child will make a beeline for your cushion or stool. The room should be airy and light even if it is small because although your eyes are closed when you pray or meditate you still need to draw in prana (life-force energy) from the air. Dark colors are not conducive to meditation as they influence your unconscious mind. If you wish to aid meditation with color, buy a purple lampshade, window blind or violet colored light bulb (see page 105). Aroma can also help raise our consciousness, aiding meditation (see page 85).

The best shape rooms are those which are octagonal, hexagonal or circular. Certain shapes in this room will also aid the peace and harmony and your ability to connect to spiritual forces. If your room is square or rectangular, you can introduce spiritual shapes. A bay window or atrium is ideal, and if your room is on the top floor, a small glass or perspex dome can bring in light and allow you to view the sky during the day and the stars at night. Many people have reported that sitting in a pyramid shape helps improve their meditation.

Create a protective spiritual shape on which to lie or sit by cutting a foam cushion or folding a cloth or blanket to your desired shape. If you wish the structure to be more permanent, build a wooden platform in the shape of a circle, hexagon, octagon or star.

Chinese 'moon gate'

Many temples and sacred places have a protective entrance, often a small opening which allows only one person to pass through at a time. These doorways symbolize the transition between the outside and internal world. Often the lintels are low, so you have to bend to enter the special space. Create a protective doorway by hanging a curtain or ornamental hanging above the door. If you are converting a loft or building, a key-hole, arched or round opening (which the Chinese call a moon gate) into your sacred space will signify a special and honored place in your home.

Gazebo

The word gazebo literally means 'to gaze'. Traditionally, gazebos were erected on a spot where you could enjoy a beautiful view. The shelter, which was not part of the house, was more like a garden room that protected you from the elements while providing you with a tranquil setting away from the house.

A favorite shape for a gazebo is octagonal, although it can also be round or square. A gazebo needs to be light and airy as well as attractive and it can create a mystical place in your garden where you can sit and contemplate or meditate.

Perfect Protection

Every home needs to provide perfect protection for its occupants. In it you need to feel entirely safe and secure from the outside world, as well as feeling protected from subtle vibrations, which can permeate your sacred space.

A family pet can raise the alarm, and having a door chain and spy hole allows you to view any caller to your home before you allow them to enter. Other early warning systems can be a gravel path, bells or wind chimes hung next to the front door. Most of us are aware of the physical precautions to take when you leave your home and it does no harm to remember that windows and doors should be well secured and fences and gates should be strong and lockable.

More subtle forms of house protection can be just as effective. Most religions and cultures have their own forms of spiritual home protectors. In the Jewish tradition, for example, a small plaque containing a prayer is fixed to the door frame when moving into a new home. This prayer asks for protection and prosperity for its occupants and is kissed each time someone enters your home. In the Middle East, a glass bead was placed somewhere on the door frame to provide protection against the evil eye.

The best way to find your personal house protector is to tune in to your intuition. Find out the form the guardian of your house wishes to take through a creative visualization or meditation. It may be an animal, object or spiritual mentor and guide.

If your house guardian is in animal or bird form, try to get a sculpture or carving of this creature to stand on either side of your front door. You may also be able to find a door-knocker to represent your house protector. If your guardian is in human form, try to create a painting or find a picture which represents this person. It may be that they are an angel, prophet or saint, in which case you might be able to buy pictures of them. If you believe that a spiritual master's human form should not be shown, use a color, animal or plant to represent the qualities of that person.

Other forms of protection

There are other ways you can help protect your home. Light can provide protection on both a physical and spiritual level. Having a garden lamp or porch light which is movement sensitive can act as a strong deterrent for would-be intruders and keeping a light on a timing device is an excellent way of protecting your home when you are away.

Color can also provide protection as it can deflect bad vibrations. The best colors for this are black or dark midnight blue. There are also the herb and flower essences which have long been known to have subtle and powerful protective vibrations (see box, right).

Take time and care to create a healing home; you will find that it will serve you well. Its spirit will radiate loving and harmonious vibrations, providing you and your family with perfect protection.

Useful Addresses

Organizations

UK

Association for the Conservation of Energy
9 Sherlock Mews
London W1M 3RH, UK

British Herbal Medicine Association
Lane House, Cowling
Keighley, W Yorks BD22 0LX, UK

British Society of Dowsers
Sycamore Cottage, Tamley Lane
Hastingleight, Ashford, Kent, UK

The Building Centre
26 Store Street, London WC1, UK

Chelsea Physic Garden
66 Royal Hospital Road
London SW3 4HS, UK

Energy and Environment Unit
Open University
Milton Keynes MK7 6AA, UK

Federation of Master Builders
33 John Street, London WC1 2BB, UK

Feng Shui Network International
Lazenby House, 2 Thayer Street
London W1M 5LG, UK

Greenpeace UK
30-31 Islington Green
London N1 8XE, UK

The Holistic Design Institute
Farfields House
Jubilee Road, Totnes
Devon TQ9 5BP, UK
Telephone: 01803 868 037
Fax: 01803 866 079
e-mail: HDI@eclipse.co.uk

International Association for Colour Therapy
IACT, PO Box 3, Potters Bar
Hertfordshire EN6 3ET, UK

Iris International
School of Colour Therapy
Farfields House
Jubilee Road, Totnes
Devon TQ9 5BP, UK

National Society for Clean Air
136 North Street, Brighton BN1 1RG, UK

Society for the Preservation of Ancient
Buildings
37 Spital Square, London E1 6DY, UK

US

American Association for Crystal Growth
PO Box 3233
Thousand Oaks, CA 91359-0233, USA

American Crystallographic Association
PO Box 96, Ellicott Station
Buffalo, NY 14205-00963, USA

American Herbalist Guide
Box 1683, Soquel, CA 95073, USA

American Holistic Medical Association
4101 Lake Boone Trail, Suite 201
Raleigh, NC 27607, USA

American Society of Naturalists
Dept of Biology
Queens College of CUNY
Flushing, NY 11367, USA

Center for Clean Air Policy
444 N. Capital Street, Suite 602
Washington DC 20001, USA

Feng Shui Guild
PO Box 766
Boulder, CO 80306, USA

Feng Shui Institute of America
PO Box 488
Wabasso, FL 32970, USA

Flower Essence Society
PO Box 459
Nevada City, CA 95959, USA

Greenpeace USA
1436 U Street NW
Washington DC 20009, USA

Lighting Research Institute
120 Wall Street, 17th Floor
New York, NY 10005-4001, USA

Natural Food Associates
PO Box 210
Atlanta, TX 75551, USA

Solar Box Cookers International
1724 11th Street
Sacramento, CA 95814, USA

Suppliers

Air Purifiers
UK

London Ionizer Centre
65 Endell Street
London WC2H 9AJ, UK

Mountain Breeze
Peel House, Peel Road
Skelmersdale
Lancs WN8 9PT, UK

US

National EnviroAlert Company
297 Lake Street
Waltham, MA 02154, USA

Purity Home Product Inc
Box 397, Milersport
OH 43046, USA

Bamboo and wicker
UK

Oxfam
272 Banbury Road
Oxford OXC2 7DZ, UK

US

Bamboo & Rattan Works, Inc
470 Oberlin Avenue

South Lakewood NJ 08701, USA
Bielecky Brothers, Inc
305 East 61st Street
New York, NY 10021, USA

Full-spectrum lights
UK
Truelite SML, Unit 4, Wye Trading Estate
London Road
High Wycombe, Bucks HP11 1LH, UK

Heating
UK
Low-energy Supply Systems
84 Colston Street, Bristol BS1 5BB, UK

Hot tubs and saunas
US
Amerec Sauna Steam
NASSCOR, Inc, PO Box 40569
Bellevue, WA 98004, USA

Jacuzzi Whirlpool Bath
PO Drawer J
Walnut Creek, CA 94596, USA

Natural fabrics
UK
The Crafts Council
12 Waterloo Place
London W1M 5LG, UK

The Sheep Shop
54 Neal Street, London WC2, UK

US
Natural Fabrics
14 E Cota Street
Santa Barbara, CA 93101, USA

Sew Natural Fabrics by Mail
Rt 1 Box 428
Middlesex, NC 27557, USA

Natural flooring
UK
The Crucial Trading Company
77 Westbourne Park Road

London W2, UK
Fired Earth
Twyford Mill, Oxford Road, Adderbury
Oxfordshire OX17 3HP, UK

Three Shires
3 Ptarmigan Place, Townsend Drive
Attleborough fields
Nuneaton, Warwickshire CV11 6RX, UK

US
Country Floors, Inc
15 East 166th Street
New York, NY 10003, USA

JL Powell & Company, Inc
600 South Madison Street
Whiteville, NC 28472, USA

Natural paints
UK
Crown Berger
PO Box 37, Crown House, Hollins Road
Darwin, Lancs BB3 0BG, UK

Farrow and Ball Ltd
24-26 Uddens Trading Estate
Wimborne, Dorset BH21 7NL, UK

Nutshell Natural Paints
Newtake
Staverton, Devon TQ9 6PE, UK

New Wool Mattresses
UK
The Fairchild Co
2a Willeton Trading Estate
Willeton
Taunton, Somerset TA4 4RF, UK

Futon Company
82/3 Tottenham Court Road
London W1P 9HD, UK

SAD and Light Therapy
UK
Outside In Ltd
Unit 21, Scotland Road Estate

Dry Drayton, Cambridge CB3 8AT, UK
Scent
UK
Neals Yard Remedies
5 Golden Cross Walk
Cornmarket Street
Oxford OX1 3EU, UK

Tisserand Aromatherapy Products
Brighton BN3 ZRS, UK

US
Aphrodesia Products
282 Bleeker Street
New York, NY 10014, USA

The Essential Oil Company Ltd
100 Enterprise Place
Dover, DE 19901, USA

Heaven's Herbal Creations
8202 West ML Avenue
Kalamazoo, MI 49009, USA

Slate, limestone, marble, granite, sandstone, terracotta
UK
Grange Mill
Raglan, Gwent NP5 2AA, UK

Sound
UK
New World Cassettes
Paradise Farm, Weshall
Halesworth, Suffolk IP19 8BR, UK

Water filters
UK
Aquastream
Scandinavian Direct Ltd, Aries House
East Grinstead, West Sussex RH19 3UG, UK

US
Action Filter, Inc
777 Wyoming Avenue
Kingston, PA 18704, USA

Bibliography

Cirlot, JE *A Dictionary of Symbols* (Philosophical Library Inc, 1962)

Cowen, Painton *Rose Windows* (Thames & Hudson, 1992)

Hargittai, Istvan and Magdolna *Symmetry: a Unifying Concept* (Shelter Publications Inc, California, 1994)

Hughes, Philip *A Need for Old Buildings to Breathe* (pamphlet)

Kron, Joan *Home-Psych* (Clarkson N Potter Inc, 1984)

Lander, Hugh *House and Cottage Conversion* (Acanthus Books)

Laporte, Caroline *High Energy Living* (Century Paperbacks, 1988)

Linn, Denise *Sacred Space* (Rider, 1995)

Marc, Oliver *Psychology of the House* (Thames & Hudson, 1977)

Mollison, Bill *Introduction to Permaculture* (Tagari Publications, 1991)

O'Brien, Joanne *Feng Shui* (Element Books, 1992)

Pearson, David *The Natural House Book* (Conran Octopus, 1989)

Society for the Protection of Ancient Buildings *Electrical Installations in Old Buildings*

Toth, Max and Greg *Pyramid Power* (Nielsen, 1988)

Wheeler, Mortimer *Roman Art and Architecture* (Thames & Hudson, 1981)

Whiton, Sherrill *Elements of Interior Decoration* (JB Lippincott Company, 1944)

Windows and Doors (Sunset Publishing, 1993)

Acknowledgements

The publisher thanks the following photographers and organisations for their kind permission to reproduce the photographs in the book:

2 The Interior Archive/Tim Clinch; 5 The Interior Archive/Henry Wilson; 6 Ianthe Ruthven; 10-11 The Interior Archive/Tim Clinch; 15 Robert Harding Picture Library/Bill Reavell/Home & Ideas/©IPC Magazines; 17 Arcaid/Willem Retthmeier/Belle; 18-19 Ianthe Ruthven; 21 The Interior Archive/Fritz von der Schulenberg; 22-23 Elizabeth Whiting & Associates/Jean-Paul Bonhommet; 26 Elizabeth Whiting & Associates/Jean-Paul Bonhommet; 30 The Interior Archive/Simon Upton; 32-33 The Interior Archive/Henry Wilson/designer Sophie Saren; 34-35 Ianthe Ruthven; 38 Arcaid/Alan Weintraub; 40-41 Paul Ryan/International Interiors/Jack Lenor Larsen; 44-45 Elizabeth Whiting & Associates/Brian Harrison; 46-47 Elizabeth Whiting & Associates/Dennis Stone; 50-51 Arcaid/Richard Bryant/Philippe and Ariane Michel/Architectes GEA, Domaine de Sperone; 53 The Interior Archive/Fritz von der Schulenberg; 55 The Interior Archive/Henry Wilson; 56 Elizabeth Whiting & Associates/Michael Nicholson; 60-61 Elizabeth Whiting & Associates/Andreas von Einsiedal; 62 Elizabeth Whiting & Associates/Brian Harrison; 68-69 The Interior Archive/Brian Harrison; 70-71 Arcaid/Alan Weintraub; 74-75 The Interior Archive/Jacques Dirand; 78-79 The Interior Archive/Simon Upton; 80-81 The Interior Archive/Brian Harrison; 84 The Interior Archive/Fritz von der Schulenberg; 86-87 Mike Newton ; 91 The Interior Archive/ Fritz von der Schulenberg; 92-95 Undine Prohl/A Lopez Baz Architect; 96-97 Michael Crockett; 99 Arcaid/Willem Retthmeier/Belle; 100 The Interior Archive/Fritz von der Schulenberg; 103 Arcaid/Alan Weintraub; 106-107 Undine Prohl/Natalye Appel Architect; 109 Elizabeth Whiting & Associates/Tom Leighton; 111 The Interior Archive/Brian Harrison; 112-113 Undine Prohl/Mockbee/Coker Architects.

Index